To Dra

SELLER BEWARE

HOW NOT TO SELL YOUR BUSINESS

ONE WOMAN'S ROAD TO RUIN

DENISE BARNES

Very best wishes

Denise Barnes

\Bᵇ\
Biteback Publishing

First published in Great Britain in 2013 by
Biteback Publishing Ltd
Westminster Tower
3 Albert Embankment
London SE1 7SP
Copyright © Denise Barnes 2013

ISBN 978-1-84954-536-5

10 9 8 7 6 5 4 3 2 1

A CIP catalogue record for this book is available from the British Library.

Set in Bembo

Printed and bound in Great Britain by
CPI Group (UK) Ltd, Croydon CR0 4YY

MIX
Paper from
responsible sources
FSC
www.fsc.org   FSC® C020471

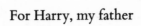

For Harry, my father

Contents

Introduction

When I started to write this book I had no idea of the ending. This is because I was knee-deep in trying to resolve a terrible situation – the result of selling my flourishing estate agency business to the *wrong buyers* and endeavouring to claim the money I was owed.

If you are a business owner, I hope that when you come to sell your business you will have read my story long before you sign on the dotted line, and will be alerted to all the mistakes I made. And if you don't own a business, and never intend to, you might be intrigued to read of one woman's road to ruin.

On the face of it, I wasn't a naïve businesswoman, though later I suppose I could have been described as such. I was the proprietor of a thriving business with a superb reputation; I had steered it through a four-year recession which began in the late 1980s, and had expanded by using my own profits. I rarely used any overdraft facilities, had built up a healthy bank balance in case of emergencies, and throughout most of my seventeen years in business I'd made an extremely comfortable living.

It was 2004. The housing market was stable; now was the right time to get the business ship-shape for sale, make my million and sail away to that magical island before I turned sixty.

Nothing could have prepared me for what happened…

I was seven years old when I first realised I could sell. My sister Anna, two years older, would knit and cut out dolls' clothes, and after she'd sewn all the tiny components together she would arrange the outfits in a cardboard tray, punch two holes and wind a piece of string through, then slip it around my neck. I used to feel like an ice-cream usherette in the cinema.

Anna loved making clothes – I loved selling them. I'd go round all the houses in the neighbourhood where they had children, heart thumping, not with nerves but at the thought of making a sale. It was rare if I came home with any items left in the tray.

When we grew out of that little venture I used to help my grandmother in her shop. She lived quite a long way away from us so we only saw her two or three times a year, but when we did, I was in heaven. Although I was only ten she allowed me to serve the customers so long as she was there to watch what I was doing. By the time I was eleven she let me take sole charge while she filled in her football coupons in the back room, or talked to one of the myriad reps who would stop by.

My grandmother had opened her own shop decades before, when it was more unusual for a woman to own a business. We're talking late nineteenth century. It was a fascinating place – an original convenience store. You name it, Nana sold it. When she first bought the cottage it would have been her front parlour, and in those days you could turn part of your home into commercial premises with no permission whatsoever.

I adored it. The very smell of it. Musty mothballs from the second-hand clothes mixed with the rancid odour of mature cheese and the warm yeasty aroma of loaves of bread, delivered daily.

My heart would start to beat faster when I opened the door

from the rest of Nana's cottage at the back and stepped into the shop. I loved tidying up the shelves and arranging the new deliveries, careful to bring forward the old stock so as to rotate it, as Nana had instructed. I loved the sound of the doorbell announcing the arrival of a customer. Best of all, I loved the surge of excitement when the customer would hand me the money and I could dive into the till and take out the change, counting it out in their palm.

I used to help myself to a few sweets now and again while reading love comics on a high three-legged stool behind the counter when trade was slow. I consoled myself with the thought that I would sometimes be there several hours so the occasional bar of chocolate, I reasoned, was perfectly justified. This was until one day Nana bustled in and caught me pinching a couple of chocs from a tin of Roses.

'You naughty girl!' She snatched them from my hand and threw them back in the tin. I blushed to my roots. 'You're eating all my profits.'

It was the first time I'd come across that concept and even though I was upset I tucked it away for future use. Tears pricked the back of my eyes and I decided there and then, at the age of twelve, that one day I would have my own little shop. And no one would be able to tell me what to do.

I must have been about fifteen when my father set up his own business in Norwich selling accounting machines and typewriters and suchlike. These days it would of course have been computers. I took a great interest in his small showroom as I hadn't forgotten that one day I would have my own shop. I clearly remember when he showed me his new stationery. On the bottom left-hand side of the sheet of paper was the silhouette of a little black cat sitting upright with its tail curled around itself.

'It's Charlie,' my father said, laughing his squeaky laugh.

Charlie was one of the nine rescued cats he'd collected over the years.

'I love it, but isn't it a bit frivolous?' I asked him, impressed but worried that my father wouldn't look professional.

'It might be,' he said, 'but I guarantee no one will forget me.'

What we would now call a logo was quite something in 1960, which was still a continuation of the rather staid '50s. But at that precise moment I knew my shop would have a black cat sign.

The many years in between were varied and my jobs were far flung; mostly I was working abroad, mainly selling. Although it was all fun it wasn't leading anywhere, so I decided to return home and study for a BA Honours Degree through the Open University. At this time I was juggling the heavy workload with a brand-new (second) husband and full-time work in an estate agency within commuting distance from London; a job my sister had found for me through the Wanted ads and said I'd be good at. She was right. I'd finally found my calling.

Unfortunately, I was in a chauvinistic environment and unprepared. My father had always instilled in my sister and me that we could do whatever we set out to do in life. Being 'limited' because we were girls was never discussed. But despite my secretary/trainee negotiator job title, I soon found that the company had no intention of training me. I was to be there as a glorified secretary, at the four male negotiators' beck and call.

On my first week the chief surveyor's secretary, Sheila, waylaid me.

'I hope you're settling in, Denise.' She smiled at me.

'Oh, yes. I'm very happy, although—' I was just going to ask her what I should do about the manager's apparent reluctance to train me when Sheila interrupted.

'So what day would you like to take the cloakroom towels home to wash?'

She must have seen my blank look and went on to explain.

'You and the other three secretaries take it in turn so it only works out once a fortnight. It's two in the Ladies' and two in the Men's.'

'What about the men?'

'What about them?'

'When is it *their* turn?' I persisted.

Now it was Sheila who was taken aback.

'It's just the girls who do it,' she said, seeming not to understand where this was leading.

'Well,' I told her, determined to start as I meant to go on, 'when the men take a turn, then so will I.'

At that, Sheila, face creasing with incredulity, and grey curls bobbing with annoyance, spun on her heel and strode off.

A couple of weeks after the towel episode I finished work, put my coat on, and said goodbye to Bob, who although not the manager was my immediate boss. I stepped out into a savage November night. The rain thrashed me as I made my way out to the car park at the back, dodging the puddles but still getting soaked in the process.

When I got to my car I noticed one of the tyres was completely flat. Bugger. I was tired and hungry and just wanted to get home. I only hoped Bob hadn't left. Squelching back to the office I saw the light still on. Good old Bob. He was still there, riffling through his hot box of clients, and looked up at my approach.

'Dear, oh dear, you do look wet. What's happened?'

'Oh, Bob, I've got a puncture, and I wondered if you could help me,' I whined just a little. 'I'm only sorry it's on the foulest night of the year.'

'Of course you know I would,' he said, looking calmly at me, 'but I'm busy this evening. I've got the towels to wash!'

‡

I'd been with the company a year when a vacancy for a negotiator came up in our office. Full of confidence I applied in writing to the senior partner for the job, telling him how I'd personally won dozens of instructions over our competitors during the year, and had clients who only wanted to deal with me. I thought a little gentle humour might endear myself to him so I ended the letter, *I hope you'll agree that I'm the right 'man' for the job*. This was in the days when female estate agents were as common as repair men who turn up on time. I heard nothing. I was completely ignored. Pretty soon I began to notice a steady stream of pimply youths coming into the office and being called upstairs to the other partners' offices. It dawned on me they were being interviewed for the vacancy.

If they hire someone less experienced than me, I thought furiously, I'll take them to a tribunal.

Several more weeks crawled by. Then one lunchtime I noticed the senior partner standing at the rear entrance to our office reading his newspaper. Time to nail him.

'May I please have a word, Mr Ramsbotham?'

He looked at me over the top of his glasses, evidently annoyed that I'd disturbed him.

'You'd better come into my office.' He read a few more lines of his paper before he folded it. I followed him to his room.

'I was hoping for an answer to my letter which I put on your desk at the beginning of last month,' I began. I paused, waiting for his response, but he just sat there. 'So I'd just like to know if I'm in the running for the negotiator vacancy in our office.'

'Oh, that,' he said. 'Yes, we're going to offer it to you.'

Just like that. No apology for not coming back to me. So when was he going to tell me? His expression was inscrutable but it didn't bother me. I was elated. I was going to wave the typewriter goodbye.

'That's marvellous news,' I said, almost forgiving him for keeping me on tenterhooks. 'What will my salary be now?'

'Exactly the same.'

'But I'm only on a secretary's pay. Six thousand pounds.'

'Your salary is to remain the same,' he repeated in a tone that said 'take it or leave it', as he ushered me out of the door.

Humiliated at the unfairness, I threw him a dark look and vowed I would use the company for the rest of my training, and then leave and work somewhere else where they'd never seen me behind a typewriter.

A few months later Anna spotted an ad (she's forever spotting ads for me) in the local paper which seemed just what I was looking for. It was a multi-branch independent company and they needed a manager for one of their village offices. I applied and was offered the position immediately. The salary was an amazing £9,000 a year (I never got an increase from my old company), plus commission, plus a car. I couldn't have been more bucked.

Because I had no valuation experience of this particular village my twinkly-eyed new boss, Paul, who was the area manager, sent Richard, one of the managers from a nearby branch, to give me some training. Richard could only spare me one morning, taking me out in his car where we zig-zagged round the village, he pointing out the various areas and the value of the houses, me desperately jotting down notes as he drove along.

He clued me in on the company, which he'd been with for

years, said they were a decent lot, and to call him whenever I needed any help. Then he dropped me outside the office and revved away.

I remember thinking at the time (thirty years ago!) what a very nice and professional estate agent he was. Little did I know Richard was to play an important part in my estate agency career.

Turning back into the office, I thought what a misnomer it was to be called a manager when all I had was one part-time secretary. Janice did four mornings a week. At half-past one she shot out of the door, leaving me to answer the phone, write up the house details, put a notice on the door that I'd be back in half an hour if someone wanted to view a house, and type the letters she hadn't had time to do. Not quite what I had in mind.

Janice was rather a character. She was extremely blonde and her favourite work outfit was a pink denim jumpsuit complete with dangly earrings and thickly applied purple eye make-up.

She was a genuinely nice person but was the proverbial round peg in the square office. She was a terrible speller, the filing was all over the place – I discovered an out-of-date cheque for £1,200 in one of the files – and the whole office was a muddle. Reluctantly, I had to let her go. It was the first time in my life I'd had to sack (yes, that was the word we used in the 1980s) someone, and I didn't enjoy it one bit.

But to survive I had to put together a strong team to increase the present stock of houses, which consisted of six. Yes, just six properties. No wonder they couldn't afford the staff. But it was a Catch-22 situation.

Things were going to have to change.

It was fun building up a dedicated team to achieve the targets

I'd set for myself. Paul hadn't given me any specific figures. He just left me to it, probably thinking I couldn't do any worse.

We were the only agents in the village, which helped, and by the end of the first year we were a team of three full-time women and had turned the office around. Paul said it had made a healthy profit for the first time in years.

It was a tiny office compared with what I was used to. There was only enough space for two desks so someone always had to stand. The poky little storage room out the back wasn't large enough for even a chair so there was nowhere we could sit and have a sandwich. I began to think about expansion now we were making some money.

Our office shared a party wall with a grocer. And Mr Trenton, the grocer, had just told me he wanted to sell. Immediately, I had the idea that my company could buy it and we could knock through to make one super-sized office. The directors could rent out the flat above, thereby having an income to offset some of the building works.

I put this to Mr Trenton.

'I want £42,000 for the freehold,' he said. (Gosh, I would have thought it would be worth more.) 'That's without the contents,' he added. Then he looked at me over the top of his glasses and said, 'I won't take anything lower and I don't want any messing about from your company. I know what these corporates are like.' He glared as though it were my fault.

During my third year the company had amalgamated with a nationwide insurance company consisting of hundreds of branches, but they'd kept on most of the people I was used to, so things hadn't changed too much, except for loads more paperwork to fill in.

'I'll tell them it's got to be the full price,' I said. 'That is, if they're interested.'

I was sure they would be.

By now I was quite excited. My boss would be so pleased with me.

The directors were very open to the idea of expanding and came down straight away to see the shop. Unbeknown to me they made him an offer. Mr Trenton told them to push off.

The offer was £25,000.

I was furious, particularly as I'd told them they mustn't make a lower offer as Mr Trenton simply wouldn't deal with them.

Later, Paul told me one of the directors had come back to Mr Trenton with a higher offer but was told in no uncertain terms they'd had their chance.

Just a few doors along the high street from where I worked was a stationery shop, and one particular day I went in to buy an emergency ream of copy paper. Eileen, who owned the business, frowned when she saw me.

'I'm very upset with your company,' she spluttered. 'They've doubled my rent. There's no way I can afford to stay here. I'll have to close.'

'It's not us who's raised the rent,' I said, 'we're only the letting agent.'

'Maybe, but they persuaded the landlord he was under-charging me.'

'How much is the rent now?' I asked idly, feeling sorry that she'd be leaving. It was handy having her there when I ran out of any office supplies.

'It's gone up to £3,000 a year.'

It sounded quite reasonable to me as I was privy to the budget for the present office, and the stationery shop wasn't much more. Plus the fact that it was three times the size and on a corner site so you could see it from across the road at all angles. But you'd have to sell a lot of notebooks and pens and pencils to pay the rent, whereas one house commission…

I rang Paul.

'I've found some new premises for the company,' I began, and told him which shop I had in mind.

'I'll get the commercial chap down to have a look,' Paul promised.

I was delighted. This time I hoped they would be serious. I just love changes. Expansions, improvements, transformations. It keeps the old adrenalin alive and kicking.

Paul and the commercial chap turned up a couple of days later and I walked with them to the stationer's. The commercial chap, an older man, didn't say much. Just sucked at his pipe. He glanced through the windows but to my disappointment didn't go inside. Well, he didn't need to really, I thought. He could see all the lovely space. Then he turned to me.

'It won't do at all, Denise.'

'Why?' I felt really stupid that I'd dragged him over for nothing.

'Just look at the location.' He swung his head towards my office. 'It's nowhere near as good as where you are now. You're in the best spot. Right opposite the zebra crossing.'

'But the zebra crossing's only twenty yards away,' I spluttered. 'You can only get two shops opposite the zebra crossing anyway.'

'Yes, and yours is one of them,' he said. 'That's why it's so good.'

'Do you honestly think someone looking for a house isn't going to walk a few yards away from the zebra crossing to see what's in the estate agent's window?' I said, not believing what I was hearing.

He took the revolting pipe out of his mouth. 'Look, Denise, you don't know what you're talking about. This is *my* field. You just get on,' he actually flicked his hand towards me as though he were waving away an irritating bluebottle, 'with selling houses. Leave the commercial side to me.'

I looked at him, barely able to disguise my contempt. And in that split second I thought: *You* don't think it would make a smashing office, but *I do*.

Here it was in front of me. An opportunity to start my own estate agency and I'd very nearly muffed it. *This village is big enough for both of us,* I heard John Wayne's drawl, making me grin in a rather stupid fashion. Trying to contain my excitement I mumbled an apology that I'd wasted their time, and escaped back to my office. I was going to put my plan into action and no one was going to stop me.

The trouble was, my husband had been made redundant at the exact same time, and he begged me not to leave.

'You've got a steady job,' he said, 'earning decent money. They think the world of you and I bet it won't be long before you're promoted to the country homes department.'

But that wasn't what I wanted.

I knew I couldn't just jump in. There was a lot of ground-work to do. I would need my bank manager to confirm he would lend me the money to finance the venture, but the most important step was to get consent from the landlord of the stationery shop to agree that I become his new tenant. And that he would allow the shop to become an estate agent. If he didn't there was no point at all in taking things further. This was the tricky bit. I'd never met him and had no financial track record of being a commercial tenant.

I nipped in to the stationers to see Eileen again and confided to her that I would like to take over the premises if she really was going to have to close. She was actually very nice about it and wished me luck.

'Who's the landlord?' I asked her.

'Mike Dawson,' she said.

'How would I get in touch with him?'

She turned at the shadow of a car outside the window. 'He's just drawing up now.'

I rushed outside in the heavy drizzle and tapped on Mr Dawson's passenger window. A broad-set, heavily bearded man with a thatch of brown hair rolled the window down and leaned over to see who this mad woman was. Then he gave me a charming smile.

'Can I have a word with you?' I asked. 'It's about taking over the shop.'

'You're going to get wet out there,' he said. 'You'd better get in the car so we can talk in private.'

I know this must sound rather odd, but it seemed a perfectly sensible thing to do. He was Eileen's landlord so he must be all right, I thought. I opened the passenger door and got in.

Five minutes later I emerged, triumphant. Even though he'd never set eyes on me before, he'd agreed that I could rent it and turn it into an estate agency provided I got the necessary permission. All we'd done was shake hands. There was nothing in writing. Business conducted in this fashion would never happen nowadays, but life was simpler then. A gentleman's agreement in 1988 was still pretty sacrosanct. Mike turned out to be the kindest, loveliest landlord of them all, becoming a friend. Eventually I bought the premises from him when he was thinking of selling one of his properties and I was keen to have the extra security and independence.

The next thing was to apply for planning permission to turn what were retail premises into offices. That is, from A1 use to

A2 use. If they said no it would stymie the whole operation. The wheels turned slowly but eventually I got permission. My fear was that any planning permission applied for, followed by the decision, was always printed in the local paper. I could only hope no one would spot it.

One afternoon Richard phoned.

'Planning permission's been given for the stationery shop near you to have office use,' he said. 'And the rumour is that it's going to be an estate agent.'

My heart stopped. Why had I thought I would get away with it before someone in the company found out what I was up to?

'Oh, that,' I swallowed, somehow managing to keep my cool. 'You know it was our company that doubled Eileen's rent, so she had to pack up. But it doesn't necessarily mean it's going to be an estate agent.'

'I bet it will be,' came his reply. 'Could be some competition for you. Well, don't say you haven't been warned.'

The next fright I had was when I took some photographs of the outside of the stationery shop as I thought they might be useful to the surveyor, and for my own records. In those days you had to hand in your roll of film to the driver from the photo lab and you'd get the photographs back the following day. But the next delivery contained only some photographs of two new houses we had just taken on our books. The stationery shop photos were missing.

Half an hour later Doreen from the next village office rang.

'Denise, why have you taken photographs of the stationery shop just along the road from you?' she demanded to know.

Bloody hell.

'Oh, I was just practising with the new camera,' I stuttered. 'Taking a few street scenes. Can you send them on to me.'

'All right,' she agreed. But she sounded suspicious.

By this time I had taken Hilary, the secretary, into my confidence. She'd complained more than once that she didn't really enjoy being part of such a huge financial institution.

'I came here because it was an independent company,' she said. 'If it all goes through, would you consider me coming with you as your secretary?'

'On one condition,' I smiled. 'That I train you as a negotiator.'

'I'll give it a go,' she said, a little nervously.

'There's only one problem,' I warned her. 'Your contract will say you can't work for anyone else within two miles. Mine says the same but I've asked three solicitors if a company is likely to take an employee to court over it. One said yes, but with difficulty, and the other two said it wasn't worth the paper it's written on. That nobody can stop a person from earning an honest living. So it's a chance you'd have to take.'

'I'll risk it,' she said, smiling.

The intention was not to tell the directors about my plans until I had signed the contract for the lease, knowing finances were in place. I was due for a yearly review and I couldn't, in all honesty, pretend I was going to continue working for them. Besides, I liked this director and felt he deserved the truth. But with my plans still very much up in the air, I was taking a huge risk with my job.

'We're very pleased with you,' Stephen began. I knew what was coming. 'And we'd like to offer you the position as manager of our country homes department. There'll obviously be a decent salary increase for you,' he smiled, happy to give me such good news.

Such a contrast to the boss of my previous company. But even so I didn't waver.

'Thank you for your faith in me,' I said. 'If you'd told me this a few months ago I would have bitten your hand off, but—'

'Don't tell me you've found another job, Denise. If so, I'm sure we can better it.'

'No, nothing like that,' I said. 'I've been really happy here. But I've decided to open my own agency.'

Both eyebrows shot up. He leaned forward, cupping his chin in his hands. 'Really? It's very different having your own business from working for someone and the security that goes with it.'

I don't think he meant to sound patronising.

'I'm sure that's true, but I won't rest until I do it. And some premises have come up.'

'Where might they be?' he asked.

'Sorry, but I can't disclose it as I haven't signed the lease yet, or got my bank loan.'

Now, his eyebrows furrowed in surprise. 'And if your landlord changes his mind? Or if you don't get a bank loan after all?'

'Then I'd have to come crawling on my hands and knees and ask for my job back.' I flashed a smile.

'And I suppose I'd be weak enough to give it to you.' Stephen returned the smile as he got up from his desk and came round to me. 'Well, I wish you *moderate* success.'

'If that's all I'll get, I might as well stay with you,' I laughed, thinking to myself: *moderate*. I'm not aiming for moderate. I'm aiming for the top. I'm going to be the first woman to have the biggest chain of estate agents in the south-east. Maybe the country. My ambition was boundless.

But of course I didn't tell him that.

'We'll soon see, won't we?' His tone was ironic.

We shook hands and he thanked me profusely for all the work I'd done in building up an extremely profitable branch. I only hoped they wouldn't find anyone really good to replace me, as I'd be operating only a few doors along.

What astounded me was that Stephen didn't ask me to clear my desk right away. After all, I had plenty of time to spread my news to potential and existing clients and persuade them to come with me. But I never did tell any clients who had their houses on our books of my plans: it just wouldn't have been right.

Now that I'd given in my notice it was vital I get my bank loan. I knew it might not be easy but I had no idea what prejudice I was up against. This is a typical conversation I had with three bank managers of the 'big five'.

'I've got six years' experience in the business, and have managed an office for the last three,' I would start off. 'And I have a five-year business plan.'

My accountant had helped me draw it up, so it was professional and comprehensive, and I was sure it would be achievable. The manager would scrutinise the plan and look fairly impressed that I was not some ditzy blonde with an airy-fairy idea. Then he'd say (and it was *always* a he), 'This looks like something we might be able to go with,' followed by, 'How much are you putting in yourself?'

And I'd say, 'Ten thousand', which sounded mammoth in 1988. At that point I only had £4,000 in savings, and I had no idea where the rest would come from. I'd calculated that I would need £20,000 to set it up.

'How much do you need to borrow?'

'Another ten.'

'That seems a possibility.'

My heart would leap in excitement. Then he would say: 'Yes, I think we could definitely do something here. Of course we would need you to put your house up for collateral.'

Then my heart would sink. My husband would never agree to that, I was sure. But I would work on him.

'And we'd need his signature.'

'Excuse me?' I'd say.

The first time I heard this was from my own bank manager. He looked up at me in surprise. 'We'd need your husband's signature.'

'Why?'

'It's the rules.'

'But he doesn't have a job. *I'm* the one who pays the mortgage and all the bills. Why would you need *his* signature?'

But it seemed he did.

However, the manager of bank number four only asked for the house to be put up. And said he would come back to me in two days with a decision. Two nail-biting days later he said yes, and my husband (after threats of divorce) finally relented and allowed me to use our marital home as collateral against the loan for my new business. He even gave me his redundancy money of £6,000, which I vowed to pay back with interest by the end of my first year.

I pinched myself. I was in business.

Hilary gave in her notice as soon as I got the loan. She told me Stephen, our boss, made her pack up and go immediately. 'I felt a bit like a criminal,' she giggled, 'but I'm thrilled to be in at the beginning of your new venture.'

Within a few months I'd trained her to be a negotiator and she repaid me by being one of the best, eventually becoming one of my town managers. Soon Elizabeth, my friend who I'd met at the estate agents where I'd completed my initial training, was made redundant. The Prudential had taken it over and the new directors simply walked in and told her and the team to pack up and go. (I have to say, I was delighted when the Pru folded six months later.) What a lucky day for me when Elizabeth joined us as secretary/administrator. The third to complete the team was Joyce, a mature lady who was the true first female negotiator in the area, and often mistaken for a secretary. Her wealth of experience was a boon.

It was all I could do not to hop up and down on the pavement when I saw my name go up over the front door that summer. I remember thinking: *I wonder how long I'll have it. Five years? Ten, before I sell?* As it turned out it was seventeen years of worry, exhaustion, headaches and tears ... countered with laughs, friendship, decent holidays, cash in the bank, generous funding of my favourite charities, and a huge dollop of satisfaction that we were really helping our clients change their lives and achieve their dreams, not to mention that I was providing employment for a large number of people. If I had to earn a living, then I couldn't think of a more fun and rewarding way to do it.

But back to those early days.

It was June 1988 – the peak of the market – when I opened the doors of my own estate agency, two days before my birthday. Can you believe I used to have a queue of would-be buyers waiting for me to open up in the mornings? Sometimes there would be two or even three people dashing in at the same time for the same house, which called for all the tact we could muster. Some of the buyers would get really heated.

'I saw it first,' one woman said, elbowing past another and rushing up to my desk.

Sometimes it ended in sealed bids.

They were incredibly exciting days.

Two months later the government stopped the double tax relief on mortgages, which was a terrible blow for young couples trying to get on the property ladder. I wondered at the time if it would have a detrimental effect on my business, but

put it to the back of my mind and concentrated on building
it up. With hard work and luck I managed an excellent first
year and was able to pay back my husband with better interest
than the going rate (at my insistence), plus the whole of the
bank loan. Out came the bubbly. But in the middle of 1989
the market went slap-bang into recession.

Three years on, at the close of 1992, I lay in bed sleep-
less, night after night, resentful that my husband was lightly
snoring happily beside me. I only had enough money in
the bank to pay my staff for one more month. At that time,
no banks were bailing out businesses that desperately needed
an injection of cash. (No change there then...)

Somehow I clung on, trying not to show the staff or clients
how near to collapse we were. Miraculously, and unexpectedly, we turned the corner: a big sale where the shaky chain
had broken down irretrievably (or so we had thought) suddenly
went through and saved our necks for the next couple of
months.

When things began to look a little brighter I opened a second
branch, though we were by no means out of the recession.

'You must be mad, or know something we don't,' several
people said.

But after a longer than usual lead-in, that office eventually
made a good profit, and over the course of another decade I
expanded to eight offices and fifty employees.

Roll forward to 2004 and a pretty stable housing market
that we glass-half-full agents predicted was about to become
'buoyant'.

The perfect time to sell.

ONE

Instructing the business agent

What came across loud and clear from the three books I bought about how to sell your business was that I needed to do a whole lot of preparation before I should even *think* about putting it on the open market. Depending upon the size and nature of the business this preparation can take anything from one to five years. No way was I going to take that long. A year would be plenty as I'd always prided myself on being pretty much on top of things. But I'd have to stay close to the three books and the advice they gave to make sure I'd done everything possible to get my business in tip-top order.

The first book was by an American author. (I chose it particularly since I had previously lived and worked in the States for many years. During that time I came to the conclusion that Americans tended to be better at marketing and indeed business than the British.) The second was by an English author, which had the benefit of describing the way we in the UK conduct our transactions. I read them both, cover to cover, twice over, highlighting chunks when I thought the advice was particularly valuable.

The third was a little pocket book called *How To Make Your First Million*, by Lillian Too. Its size, about that of a CD, and dull gold cover attracted me, and I thought it would be fun to be the first millionaire in the family. It was written more as a narrative, though crammed with excellent tips – that is, until I got to the end section. The strong advice there was that I should feng shui my office in order to enhance my road to success. I didn't believe in feng shui one little bit. In fact, whenever a Chinese family came into my office looking to buy, they drove me nuts when so many properties I showed them which were perfect for their needs faced, according to them, the wrong way.

'It doesn't allow the evil spirits to escape down the toilet,' one husband told me, his face deadpan.

I re-read Ms Too's last section. She'd been amazingly success-ful in selling and buying up businesses. She was a millionaire many times over. So I thought maybe I should give it a go.

The first thing she advised me to do was to change my signa-ture if it didn't slope the right way. If you wanted to 'attract success and prosperity', she said, your signature needs to 'start with a firm upward stroke and end with another firm upward stroke'. Oh, dear. We'd struck the first problem. I have a differ-ent signature from one signing to the next. This is because I was diagnosed fifteen years ago with focal hand dystonia, a neurological disorder which means the brain, without much warning, doesn't send the correct signals to your writing hand. My bank manager had only just got to grips with all these different signatures, so not a good start, if Ms Too had anything to say about it.

Moving the furniture would be more easily accomplished.

But what on earth would Elizabeth, my PA, say when I told her we were going to feng shui the office so that the business would be more prosperous? She was a down-to-earth person and would think I'd gone 'cuckoo', to use her expression. Book in hand, before Elizabeth came in, I looked around my office.

Ms Too warned you must never sit at a desk with your back to the door as you would likely 'get cheated, taken for a ride or stabbed in the back'. Oh, dear. Every day I'd been sitting, none the wiser, with my back to the door just waiting for the knife. She suggested several areas where other furniture should be placed, all of them different from my present arrangement, and stressed the importance of living plants and fish tanks, placed correctly, which would help find the right buyer.

I decided it was all mumbo jumbo but I'm sure Ms Too, and any Chinese readers, would probably tell me that this was my big mistake – to ignore feng shui at my peril.

I know, however, that my first mistake was made at my first port of call: the business selling agent.

An agent who sells businesses should not be thought of as doing a similar job to an agent who sells houses, or any other kind of agent for that matter. True, there are things in common, such as matching people with a house, a job, a holiday, or even a date, but selling a business is much more complex. We tend to think of a house as being a person's biggest financial asset but anyone who has ever sold a business will have much more at stake. Often the business is worth considerably more than the owner's house, and in almost every case (and certainly in mine) the graft, worry, responsibility and emotion which you have ploughed into your business, not to mention the money invested, is a hundred times more than you would ever normally exert in your home. So it is vital to choose the right agent who understands *your* kind of business. It is also important that there is a rapport between you as you will be working closely together throughout the process and eventual transaction. It goes without saying that there must be absolute trust.

I had discovered a company three years before when they

had sent me an invitation to attend one of their seminars. It was held one evening in a hotel in a town far enough away for me to think that no one would know me. I managed to resist the idea of going with a brown paper bag over my head, and instead twisted my hair up and played down the lipstick. My cover, however, was blown in the first five minutes when a tall figure, somewhere in his fifties, strolled up to me and said: 'Hello, Denise. I thought I recognised you.'

Damn. Just what I didn't want: word to get round that I was going to sell. But worse was that I couldn't remember his face let alone his name, so I had no idea if he would blab or not.

'Gosh, it must be years since I last saw you,' I said, bluffing madly, hoping he'd throw me a clue or two.

'Not that long,' he said, squinting at me. 'We sat next to each other at the Chamber lunch only a few weeks ago.'

Double damn.

'Oh, of course.' I still didn't remember who he was.

'So you're thinking of selling the empire?'

'Just gathering information,' I said. 'I think these seminars are a good way to remind you of all the jobs you need to do before you actually go on the market, don't you?'

'Definitely.' He wiped his forehead. Maybe he was equally worried.

'But I'm not selling for years yet,' I said, desperate that he shouldn't draw the wrong conclusion. 'They say you should look at your exit strategy at least five years before you intend to sell, so that's what I'm doing.'

'Yes, me too.'

We chatted a few minutes longer and, wanting to bring it to a close, I said, 'Have you got a business card?' I still had no idea who the devil he was.

'Sorry, I didn't bring any with me,' he said apologetically. 'But I'm in the phone book.'

Thanks, pal.

I managed to excuse myself and talk to some people I didn't recall ever meeting before, and to my relief it soon became clear that not everyone was planning on selling that year. Or that's what they were telling me anyway.

The selling businesses company seemed to be a pretty slick operation, and I was impressed with the speakers who made sense and who patently enjoyed their job. After the event they handed me a brochure which I put by until the time was right. Now I had made my decision I called their nearest office. I also had the names of another two companies to get a feel of which one was the most suitable – the same as you would have two or three agents give you a valuation when you came to sell your house.

Alan Dorrinne sounded friendly, professional and enthusiastic, inspiring confidence straight away, and was pleased I'd attended one of his company's seminars. He usually operated in another county but said it wouldn't be inconvenient for either of us as he was used to driving over a large territory so could easily see me. I could just as easily get the train when I had to see him and he could pick me up at the station and take me to his office.

You might wonder why I didn't choose a local business agent. There were several in the area but I thought this time I would have an agent out of town. I'd tried the process of selling five years before, using a local agent, and too many people found out about it. You only need one secretary in the solicitors' office to tell her husband (even though they are supposed to be sworn to secrecy) for word to get around, and suddenly you have your employees hunting in the Wanted ads. I didn't want this to happen when I was now dead serious.

We arranged to meet in the coffee lounge of a local hotel – well, local to me. I'd brought all my paperwork with me and a brief description of the various offices, the staff, and the income over the last five years. (Businesses usually have to produce five years' worth of accounts prior to the sale.)

Alan walked in. Several women in the lounge looked up. And drooled. Including me. You rarely got anyone this gorgeous walking about in our village. He was the proverbial tall, dark and handsome with a winning smile. It won me over in a heartbeat.

He ordered a pot of coffee and hot milk (just how I like it) and his easy manner ensured that we talked like old friends. It's my usual manner when I've given a vendor a valuation on their home and then encouraged them to give me formal instructions to go ahead. Even though I realised what he was doing I still fell for it. (You probably know that a salesperson can sell to another salesperson easier than anyone else. I've often wondered if it's the sympathy factor – feeling sorry for the one who's trying to make a sale, as we salespeople picture ourselves in their hopeful position.) He asked all sorts of questions about the business; he assured me that his company had sold firms of estate agents before, and that he would do a great job of achieving the best possible price.

'Talking about price, how much are you hoping to achieve?' he suddenly said.

Even cocooned in my caffeine-induced glow, the mention of what my business might be worth made me focus on the reason why we were having this cosy chat. Good-looking or not, Mr Alan Dorrinne would have to brave a valuation without any prompting from me.

'That's what I want you to tell *me*.'

He scrutinised the figures again. 'I'm thinking around £1.75 million,' he said, watching my expression.

This was way beyond my wildest calculations, not to mention my dreams. I'd hoped for maybe £1.25 million but wondered even then if I was being realistic.

'I'm not sure that's achievable, but it would be brilliant if it came anywhere close,' I blurted, my heart practically leaping out of my chest.

'Well,' said Alan, relaxing back in the leather armchair, 'that will give us some leeway. You might have to settle at 1.5.'

Goodness, I'd lost a quarter of a million in less than thirty seconds, but, again, I was used to dealing with clients who wanted too much for their properties and if Alan had valued my estate agency at £1.75 million, losing a quarter of a million was almost a technicality. Still, I wish I hadn't let him know what an easy client (or do I mean pushover?) I would be at such an early stage. I made a mental note to be more circumspect in future.

Alan topped up my coffee and treated me to another of his charming smiles.

A business agent will love it if you're prepared at the onset to take a lot less than the figure they've recommended as it will, of course, be easier to attract a buyer and they will get their commission sooner. You need to draw on your business experience in order to follow the procedures in selling your business but you should also seek professional advice, such as an accountant, to help you gauge as accurately as possible what it's worth. The correct valuation of your business is crucial, as if it's too high you won't get any takers and if it's too low you'll be selling it short. Best of all is a figure pitched at a reasonably robust level and you would hope to have more than one person interested so they compete against each other. Just like selling property, I thought. If only all this had gone through my mind *before* the meeting.

'What are your terms?' I asked Alan.

Without missing a beat he said, 'Five per cent of the eventual selling price.'

Ouch!

'And my clients grumble at me when I tell them our fees are 1.5,' I said, quite shocked.

'There's a lot of expensive advertising, long meetings, finding out about the background of potential buyers, getting involved with solicitors, negotiating on your behalf, and so on.'

Quite frankly, it didn't sound any more complicated than when I sold a house. I thought of all the times my clients had persuaded me to reduce my commission, so I bluntly asked, 'Is that the best you can do?'

He gave the impression of thinking for a moment or two (he'd obviously worked out what he was going to say if this question came up), and after scribbling down a few calculations said, 'What about 3.5 per cent up to the first million, and 5 per cent on anything over?'

I readily agreed as I've been known to come up with this kind of formula myself. I have since learned that this is still a very high percentage for a business of my sort of size, but at the time I was more than happy to pay as Alan's valuation was so much better than I'd expected.

Alan rapidly filled in some boxes on an official-looking pad of forms.

'So if you'd like to read this through and if you're happy with it, sign along the bottom,' Alan said, handing me three pre-printed pages.

I can't believe I read it in front of him. Common sense should have told me to take it home and read it quietly, sleep on it, and still refrain from signing until I'd talked to a couple of other similar companies to get their valuations, services and fees, as I'd initially planned. Instead, I was carried away by a charming agent, forgetting any business sense as I signed on the dotted line right there and then.

He must have driven off in his car punching the air.

Although I was to go down such a rocky road when I sold my business I would still strongly recommend employing the services of an agent rather than trying to save money to 'do it yourself'. And if you have a sizeable business you absolutely *must* use an agent. You tend to get a better price as the agent will reach hundreds more potential buyers than you could, and they are trained to be tough negotiators.

Don't forget business agents charge a percentage of the negotiated price so every £10,000 extra they can squeeze from a buyer gives them a better commission. Rather than being resentful that the agent is making all that extra money, remember it's ultimately good news for *you* as you will make a *lot* more.

And finally, the agent will keep your name anonymous in all the advertising until someone comes along who shows serious interest. Before going any further the potential buyer will have to sign a confidentiality agreement in order to gain access to your accounts. At that point the agent might still not disclose your name. If it leaks out that you're selling you'll find you'll unsettle the staff – the last thing you want if you get halfway down the selling road and the buyer either pulls out or you decide the deal is not as good as you had first thought and call it off.

Checklist:

1. Rather than instruct anyone at the initial interview get at least two, preferably three, valuations (any more will be confusing), and think about it for a day or two. Do some background checks and ask if you can speak to any previous clients. Weigh up which agent you feel most comfortable with and which one is giving you sensible rather than inflated figures. Only then instruct a firm or individual.

2. Choose the business agent based upon their track record, expertise, cost and service provided.

3. If you feel uncomfortable with them in any way, even if you've already instructed them and it's further down the line, don't hesitate – ditch them.

4. Wait until the agent suggests an asking price before revealing your hand. Have your accountant give their estimate, so you have a realistic idea.

5. Negotiate the best possible terms on the agent's commission. There may be bigger reductions possible than those first offered.

6. Look closely at the terms and conditions before signing. Scrutinise the small print. It may say you will have to pay fees on the whole amount of the asking price even if that figure is not achieved. If this is the case, ask for the wording to be altered so you are not paying the agent on a figure or percentage that never materialises.

7. Always read the contract quietly, on your own or with a member of the family. And be extra wary if the agent says he is willing to reduce the commission if you sign immediately. (My agent didn't suggest any such thing but I have heard more than once that some estate agents do this, so I am sure it's not beyond a business selling agent.) It would be completely unethical, so beware, even if the discounted commission is tempting.

TWO

Meeting the interested parties

At last, after Alan had been advertising my business for about a month, there was a response and he arranged for four parties to sign the confidentiality agreement.

Alan wanted me to meet all of them. I was surprised, having understood that initially he would give them a private interview to get some idea as to their expertise on running my little empire; whether they were serious, and to confirm their financial status. Also, he needed to make sure they were prepared to pay the full price (or something close to it) before they met me so as not to waste our time. Furthermore, I was reluctant to give away my identity at such an early stage. Surely that was what I was paying him for? But Alan encouraged me to be there at the first meeting.

'It's right they should meet you and get a real feel for the business,' he said. 'And no one knows that better than you.'

'I'd rather keep a distance until you've found out more about what they're looking for. It might not be right for them. And whether they can come up with the funds.'

'At this stage I think it's more important for you to form an opinion,' Alan said. 'You might get a gut reaction on something that escapes me.'

I was flattered that he wanted me there but, in hindsight, I should have listened to my instincts.

‡

The first gentleman we spoke to, Anthony Bradshaw, was very pleasant and seemed serious about buying my sort of business. I liked him straight away. He was smartly dressed, in his forties, had angular, intelligent features, thinning brown hair and hazel eyes that sparkled with enthusiasm. His background was buying businesses, normally when they were floundering, breaking them up, improving them, and selling them individually, thereby making a pile more money than the various elements would have made as one company.

I wasn't that keen to see my homogeneous whole split up and was relieved when he told me he had always wanted an estate agency business and thought my territory ideal. The branches would all remain under one company. We got along famously and even took the same train back to London together. He said it wouldn't be long before we heard from him, and I was sure he'd make an offer.

The following day I was in a London hotel taking a course about marketing, and after the last session of the afternoon the receptionist handed me a folded sheet of paper. It was a note to call Alan as soon as I got a chance.

What should I do? It wasn't exactly private where I was standing by the reception counter, and the hotel foyer was busy. Even if there was no one in the Ladies' someone was bound to come in. But my curiosity overruled my concern and I tucked myself into a corner and pulled out my mobile.

'We've heard from Anthony Bradshaw,' Alan said without any preamble. He sounded matter of fact though I could tell there was an underlying excitement.

'And?' I was glad he couldn't see me hopping up and down.

'He's made an offer.'

'Well, he hasn't wasted any time, has he?' If I wasn't holding the mobile I'd be clapping my hands. 'What's he offered?'

'I'm going to fax it through to the hotel and I want you to read it carefully. Then call me back and we'll discuss it.'

'I might not be able to call back until tomorrow morning,' I said, disappointed he was being so mysterious. 'I'm not anywhere where I can have a private conversation.'

'That's fine. I'll expect a call tomorrow.'

I gave Alan the fax number and we hung up. He hadn't hinted as to whether it was a good offer or not. I suppose that was all part of his strategy.

It was a full twenty minutes before the receptionist confirmed my name and handed me a typed sheet of paper. I skimmed over it, spotting a figure of £1.2 million, £1 million to be paid up front and the other £200,000 in stage payments. Although this was a lot less than Alan's initial valuation I thought it wasn't too bad. Worth sleeping on.

Bleary-eyed the next morning having barely slept a wink, I rang Alan before I went into work.

'What do you think?' he asked.

'It's not as much as we expected,' I started, but Alan interrupted.

'What I like about it is a whole million up front,' he said. 'I wasn't expecting anything like that.'

'Yes,' I agreed, 'but we don't want to jump at the first offer, do we? He's the only one we've seen, and we've got three others to interview.'

'They may not be interested, or they may not make such a good offer, or you may simply not like the individual,' Alan argued, a little to my surprise. When I negotiated on clients' houses, I never recommended the seller to accept the first offer. Unless, of course, it was for the full price.

I thought quickly. At this point I should have given myself

more time and insisted that we see the other contenders. But I could sense Alan didn't want to lose this chap.

'I don't want to sound desperate,' I said. 'If he'll raise his offer just a bit, say, to 1.3, I would accept.'

I almost heard his sigh of relief that I hadn't mentioned anywhere near the 1.75.

'I'll go back to him with your suggestion and phone you later.'

Every day that went by was another day with no contact from Anthony Bradshaw or Alan. I became more and more fed up, checking my mobile every hour to see whether I'd missed a call. Was this Mr Bradshaw playing games? This is how my clients must feel, I thought, when they were waiting for an offer on their house.

A week passed before we heard from him. It wasn't the news I'd been hoping for. He'd completely revised his offer by insisting that any houses which had already exchanged contracts after he had completed the purchase of my business would be his. No way, buddy. This is secure money as far as estate agents are concerned. The law says we are due our commission on the exchange of contracts, which covers the rare occurrence when the purchaser fails to complete. The staff and I would have done all the work, so I wasn't prepared to give up what amounted to £150,000 worth of commission. Also, he said if the business didn't do as well as I'd forecasted he would *deduct* money at the proportionate rate. So instead of increasing he was actually offering a much worse deal.

If Alan had recommended me to accept such terms my faith in him would have severely wobbled. But he said I should refuse it. He felt if the chap was mucking me about at such an early stage, then he might be trouble all the way.

We saw the other prospective buyers but we didn't feel any of them were suitable. One of them, a rather arrogant man, again beautifully dressed, came back with an offer of £600,000. He said he was serious but that on looking at the figures over the last five years he had come to the conclusion it wasn't worth more than that. I had great pleasure in politely telling him not to waste our time. He increased another £50,000 but I told Alan to tell him it was insulting and, unless he came up with a figure based on the asking price, I wasn't interested. The other two candidates were patently lacking in experience or funds, or both, and we never heard from them again.

More weeks went by and I was getting worried. No one else who'd enquired on the original list wanted to take their interest any further. I began to wonder if I'd been too hasty turning down Anthony Bradshaw's revised offer. I was certain my company would do as well as, if not better than, I'd anticipated so my payments in all likelihood wouldn't be eroded. Then I thought of the £150,000 worth of exchanges which Mr Bradshaw had confirmed was part of the new offer and I was annoyed. He would basically be giving me back my own money. No, the exchanges were not ever going to be part of any deal unless I got full price. Then I'd gladly throw them in.

'Where do we go from here?' I asked Alan.

He said he'd advertised it in all the right periodicals and had emailed people on his mailing list who were looking for my size of business. I trusted him to spend enough on advertising to produce a buyer as he (like estate agents) only got paid on results.

The silence was unnerving. I would phone Alan every so often but he never had any news for me, and simply said he'd call the minute he heard anything.

I threw myself into the day-to-day running of the business,

telling myself it would happen when the time was right. Meanwhile I was responsible for forty-seven women and three men, who made a team of managers, negotiators, secretaries, co-ordinators, my PA, and the general manager.

The male to female ratio may seem a little unbalanced to you, but I'd had my fill of male staff. At one point I had thirty-five women working for me and not one man. Several people began to warn me that I was going against the regulations so I thought I'd better make some enquiries. I phoned the council and asked to be put through to Equal Opportunities. I spoke to a very nice man and without giving him my name said, 'I run a business with all women and I wondered what the cut-off point is when I would have to employ a man.'

'How many women?' he asked.

'More than thirty. Half a dozen in each office. But there's only one toilet in each.'

'I'm afraid you can't use that as an excuse,' he said.

My heart sank. Oh, dear. I'd better employ some chap quickly, however unsuitable, so I can truthfully say we're an equal opportunities company.

His next words took me by surprise.

'But you can employ a thousand women and not one man and not break the law.'

'Really?'

'Yes, so long as you can prove that you treat men and women equally at the interview and employ the woman because her credentials are superior to the man, and not just because she's a woman. If you did that you'd be discriminating against men, which would be breaking the law.'

'It wouldn't make sense to do that,' I said. 'I would always employ the best *person* for the job. It's just that so far the men who've applied haven't measured up to the female applicants.

But if a man came for an interview and he was good – on paper, anyway – of course I'd employ him.'

'So you're OK then,' he said. 'But it might be prudent to keep a record of the applications and the interviews.'

Naturally over the years the odd male (and several of them were odd) would apply to work for me. Unfortunately, I'd had to sack three male managers in quick succession during the last couple of years before the sale of the business. The first had never worked in the area before but refused to take due notice of Joyce, the senior negotiator who had been with me for fifteen years, and knew practically every house in the village. She would try to advise him on the price before he went to the valuation, but he seemed to pluck figures out of the air: way over or way under. That office very nearly didn't survive.

The second one was running his own estate agency business on my computer, on my time, in my area, even using my equipment to print out the invoices.

I replaced him with a third chap. A few weeks later a woman phoned me. This manager had been to her farmhouse to give her a valuation, and she complained that he'd twice interrupted the visit to talk on his mobile. She could tell he was arranging a date. When I spoke to him about it he admitted he belonged to a dating agency and didn't want to lose any opportunity. I'm sorry, but he had to go.

Everyone in that department seemed relieved as they said he wasn't up to the job anyway. The secretary then divulged that he'd made her a rather unusual request. He'd asked her to take a photograph of him, but just a close-up of the lower part of his face. She was slightly concerned about this request but felt she was too new to say anything given he was her immediate boss, so she took the photograph. She said he asked her to take several, and every time she was ready to press the button he gave a terrifying grin. It transpired that the latest woman he wanted to meet had asked him if he had his own teeth: apparently, he'd assured her he did, but she said she wanted proof!

It did give us all a good belly laugh that afternoon.

Patrick, the general manager and one of the few males left in the company, seemed an easy chap to handle. He was very likeable and efficient and we got along well. But behind my back he boasted to Elizabeth that his job was a doddle and really only part-time. She only told me this after the sale of the business.

'Why didn't you tell me earlier?' I asked, belatedly annoyed with him.

'Because you relied on him and seemed to really like him and I didn't want to cause any trouble.'

I must say that sometimes I used to wonder where he'd disappeared to. Or he'd say to me at about four o'clock, 'If there's nothing more you want me to do I'll shoot off.'

I would look pointedly at my watch as his hours were from 9 a.m. to 5.30 p.m., but he'd say, 'I'm all up to date, so I'll see you tomorrow.'

He'd often have a long lunch but it wasn't until he'd been with me several months before I realised he regularly sloped off to the local gym. I decided to turn a blind eye. He kept up with all the work I gave him and was often ahead of me, so I didn't really have cause to complain.

But this sort of thing never happened with the women I employed. Almost without exception they were loyal, hard-working, conscientious, excellent at their job and loved having a laugh. There were rarely any cross words between them. I wouldn't have stood for it. My rule had been to set up a company that *I* would be happy to work in. Many of the girls socialised with one another outside work. I knew about their lives and their families and their personal problems. The only snag was that the younger ones would sometimes get pregnant.

'You never seem happy for us when we tell you we're pregnant,' one of my best negotiators once remarked as she finished telling me she was going to have a second baby. I'd already patiently gone through a year waiting for her to come back to work from having her first child, and the (male) replacement had not brought in anywhere near the instructions she had.

'You have to look at it from my point of view,' I sighed. 'I'm trying to run a business to keep fifty people employed. I have to think of the welfare and wellbeing of *all* of you. And that includes anyone on maternity leave. Every time one of you gets pregnant it puts a strain on the office. Then I have a big headache finding a substitute for a year until they come back to work. Good negotiators aren't walking the streets. If they are, they want longer than one year's employment.'

The said employee went a bit quiet. And I hadn't mentioned that the employee on maternity leave never wants to return to full-time work, so I'm always faced with having to find another part-timer to job-share with her.

Even though I knew they enjoyed working for me, they thought I was a hard-nosed businesswoman who preferred a career to a family. It was far from the truth but I never told them otherwise.

The headache surrounding maternity leave was one of the reasons I liked hiring middle-aged women, as well as the fact that they were of the 'old school': conscientious, reliable and rarely sick. But we had a good mix and they were a super bunch.

It was awful not being able to tell the staff what I was planning. I just had to get the right person to buy who would appreciate them and keep them all on. It would be devastating if even one person lost their job.

Other things were occupying my mind. After a series of worrying symptoms, Mum had been diagnosed with cancer. It was a terrible blow as she'd survived breast cancer twenty-seven years before. She began to lose weight and look tired and drawn. I longed to have more time to spend with her but I was so bogged down in the business. And my weekly migraines were getting worse. My sister, Anna, who was my Residential Lettings Manager (and also suffered from regular migraines), thought it time we both changed direction, and she was the first in the family to encourage me to sell the business.

It's an awful thing to admit, but I often felt I simply couldn't handle it all. It had got out of my control. I'd created a monster. I was obviously in a highly emotional state and all I could think was: *I absolutely must sell this year.*

Then one morning, out of the blue, I had a call from Alan.

'I've got some news at last,' he enthused. 'I've just spoken to a Nigel Zennerming who's extremely interested in acquiring an estate agency company in partnership with his friend, Colin Dixtrow. We've been on the phone this last hour.'

'Where are they from?'

'Next county up from you,' Alan said.

Apparently, this Nigel Zennerming was asking Alan all the right questions and seemed happy with the answers Alan provided.

'So we need to set up a meeting,' Alan went on. 'They'd like to see you next Tuesday. They've suggested lunch.'

'Is that date OK with you?' I asked.

'I think you should go on your own. They'll be more likely to talk and you'll learn more than if I was there.'

'I think the two of us should be there, Alan. After all, I've never met them.'

'I can't make it,' he said. 'Besides, I've had the initial talk. I get the feeling they want to meet you on your own.'

I felt very let down. After all, he'd attended the four other meetings. He knew better than me how to sell businesses, yet he was letting me loose on an interview with two unknown men and giving me no professional guidance. To be properly balanced – two of them, two of us – Alan should definitely be there to answer questions and gauge their intent. But he was obviously an experienced business agent who knew what he was doing, so I didn't think I should make a fuss.

'I've given Nigel Zennerming your number,' he finished, 'so you should hear from him soon.'

A few hours later Mr Zennerming duly rang me. He sounded nice, easy to talk to, and suggested he and Colin Dixtrow take me for lunch at a fish restaurant in town. By then I felt better about going on my own and began to look forward to meeting them.

At the agreed time I walked into the restaurant and there at the bar were two men, smiling at me.

'Nice to meet you,' we all said to one another as we shook hands and introduced ourselves. Both pleasant-looking men with dark hair, Colin was the taller of the two, and bearded. They looked to be around fifty years old, which I thought was perfect. I didn't want anyone too young and inexperienced or too old that they wouldn't stay with the company for very long. Both were smartly suited, shoes polished and suchlike. But then a tiny thought caught me unawares. They looked ever so slightly spivvy. Maybe it was the cerise-coloured shirt with matching spotted handkerchief in the top pocket of Nigel's jacket that raised a doubt. Or was it Colin's too-ready smile? Surreptitiously, I glanced down at their feet. Not a white sock in sight. I told myself I was being ridiculous.

'Would you like a nice chilled Chablis with the fish?' Colin asked me.

I hesitated. This was too important. Wine at lunch goes to my head much quicker than in the evening, especially as I'm not a big drinker anyway. He cocked his head on one side waiting for my reply. Why not? It might relax me. I felt strangely nervous, knowing a lot was riding on this meeting.

'That would be lovely.'

As we chatted over a delicious lunch they came across as intelligent and easy-going. There was much joking and laughter and wine (though only the one glass for me) on that first meeting. Colin used any excuse to pat my arm when he wanted to make a point or agree with me.

Was it just the wine that made Colin a shade flirtatious? I remember thinking it wasn't quite appropriate on a first meeting but chose to ignore it. I told myself it was refreshing to deal with a couple of chaps who weren't stuffy. Why shouldn't selling a business be fun for both parties? But deep down a little voice was telling me to tread with caution. I ignored it. I wanted a sale. And I could see these two buying it. And I had the feeling over just one lunch.

Nevertheless, the thought nagged me that had Alan been there he would have kept it far more businesslike. His presence would have sent out a professional message to the two men. I could have told him my concerns about their slick appearance and behaviour and see if he'd thought the same.

At the end of the lunch as the three of us were sipping our coffee, I asked, 'Are you both really serious about buying my business?'

Without even giving each other a glance or a nod they gave me a unanimous 'yes'.

I couldn't have been more delighted.

'We'll call Alan in a few days when we've had the chance to discuss it and talk to our wives,' Nigel told me.

We shook hands, Colin holding mine a little too long. Like some Mills & Boon hero, I thought, wanting to giggle. We parted company and I remember returning to the office very excited and certain Colin and Nigel were going to make an offer.

I was on tenterhooks for the next few days. Elizabeth kept looking at me with a question in her eyes. She knew me so well. She could tell I was up to something and I could feel her disappointment and hurt that I was carrying on as usual, but I was terrified to confide in anyone, even Elizabeth, my most trusted employee and loyal friend. I didn't want anyone to raise any doubts about my decision to sell.

Finally, Alan rang; he had heard from Colin and Nigel. They were going to make an offer and would be in touch in the next week or two after working out their finances.

'Are they definitely going to have it?' Mum asked, her face white and drawn with her illness. She knew how tired I was and badly wanted me to retire.

'My goal is to be sold up by my sixtieth birthday,' I told her.

That date was looming.

She smiled her beautiful smile, her eyes the brightest blue in such a pale face, as she squeezed my hand.

Checklist:

1. The confidentiality agreement is a positive step forward for you and any purchaser, so be sure your agent has found out their backgrounds, what kind of business they run or have experience of, and of course their financial status, before disclosing your company's name. The confidentiality agreement also gives buyers access to your accounts so you do have to be sure of a trust that often hasn't had a chance to build.

2. Insist that your selling agent is with you in every aspect of the process, including the initial interviews. They are not emotionally involved and will therefore be a better judge of character. This is partly what you are paying them for.

3. If you are under emotional pressure, if a member of the family is ill or some other crisis is taking up your time, it would be wise to postpone the sale for a few months, or however long is necessary. You will then be in a calmer frame of mind to concentrate on the transaction.

4. Think carefully for a few days before accepting the first offer, no matter how tempting. Other offers might come in later that are better, or other buyers' backgrounds are more relevant to the business you are selling, therefore giving you more confidence.

5. Discuss the offer at length with your agent to make sure it doesn't include any premises or other assets you own which have not been made clear in the offer. If it's genuine the buyer won't mind waiting, within reason, for a response.

6. Don't ignore gut feelings, instincts, first impressions – they're often right.

7. Ensure your agent has vetted any prospective buyers to confirm their financial status *before* they sign a confidentiality agreement.

8. Stay absolutely businesslike from the start when meeting any prospective buyers and maintain your professionalism at all times.

9. Stick to non-alcoholic drinks at all business meetings. You need a clear head.

THREE

They must mean business

Three weeks passed and I was beginning to have doubts. Surely they should have been on the phone to make an offer, even if it was a low one, to show me they were serious. I rang Alan.

'Don't worry,' he told me. 'They'll come back. I've had a very positive conversation with Nigel and he says they hope to put in an offer very soon.'

I had to be content with that. But the silence was beginning to get to me.

Sure enough, a few days later Alan rang to tell me he'd heard from them. It was another telephone conversation but they had talked over figures and conditions and had asked Alan to run it by me, and if in essence it looked viable they would put it in writing.

Their offer was £1 million to include the only office that was freehold, which I owned. Half a million up front and the rest in quarterly payments over the next three years in proportion to the income. The exchanges would be 100 per cent mine, as I'd always stipulated, but the 'under offer' pipeline would be divided between both parties, the proportion depending on how close to exchange each transaction was.

'The premises are definitely out of the equation,' I told

Alan. 'No way would I sell them. They're worth far more to me. And quite frankly, the whole package is not enough.'

'I'll go back to them,' he said. 'See if I can squeeze any more out of them.'

These were the exact words I used when discussing a low offer with one of my clients selling their house.

'What do you think of only half the money up front?' I asked.

'I'm not happy with it but they said they couldn't do more. I did try.'

'Well, I'm not happy with a million,' I said. 'It's only just over half your valuation.'

He didn't comment.

There were no other offers. The first chap, Anthony Bradshaw, seemed to have disappeared from the scene and Mum was getting worse. I was desperate to sell. I also thought that if the quarterly payments were based on the income over the next three years, then maybe with my input and all the contacts I had, I could increase the final figure so long as the market held up. I didn't give a thought as to whether the two of them would be competent to run such a business. If I had, I would naturally have assumed that would have been Alan's department.

Alan said it had to be my decision and to be fair he didn't push me to accept, but he did warn me that I might not get a better offer. If I'd valued a country house at £1.75 million I would have been too embarrassed to persuade the seller to accept such a reduction. They would certainly have lost confidence in me and my initial valuation. But maybe selling businesses was different. I thought it over. I liked Colin and Nigel and felt I could work with them, having resigned myself to the fact that I would have to work part-time in the business for at least the first year so they could learn the ropes.

My main concern was that neither of them had any estate agency experience. Nigel had told me he was a chartered surveyor who had been attached to an estate agency in London for sixteen years, so I thought he must have picked up the basics through osmosis if nothing else. Colin said he had recently sold a business about the same size as mine, selling mechanical components, whatever that was. Frankly, it sounded too dull to enquire.

After only giving it a day or so, and talking it over with my family, I decided to go ahead so long as we left the freehold building out of the equation.

Because I'd accepted the offer in principle it was time for me to meet the 'boys' (as I called them) again. They were delighted we were progressing and we chatted over another lunch about the way it would work – although we mostly talked about things that were nothing to do with the business. I learned they'd been friends for several years and had decided they would like to work in partnership in a business. And they didn't want to build one up from scratch.

'We'd set our hearts on an estate agency with a few branches,' Colin explained, 'so in time we can even expand. See it grow. What would you think if we did that?'

'I'd be very proud and delighted,' I said without hesitation. 'Particularly if I'm still involved.'

'Well, we'd all gain so it'd be a win-win situation,' Colin grinned.

It sounded perfect.

They ended the lunch by explaining that they were exploring

various banks and financial institutions to borrow the money
and they hoped to get back to me in a week or so.

'Presumably you have some collateral?' I said, feeling a little
concerned that I might be treading on Alan's toes.

'We've both got our houses,' Colin told me, 'and a fair
amount of savings, so we shouldn't have too much trouble
getting the finance.'

When we stood to say goodbye they both insisted I kiss
them on the cheek. I thought it was slightly too friendly too
quickly but didn't want to snub them, they were so smiley. I
tried to ignore Colin's prickly beard.

I reported to Alan that the meeting had gone well and they were
only waiting for a finance company to back them. Meantime,
I was wondering when would be the best time to tell Patrick,
the general manager, I was going to sell. And that I'd actually
accepted an offer. I felt it only fair to give him some warning,
though I had advised Colin and Nigel that they should keep
him on as he was the only person besides myself who knew the
nuts and bolts of the business, though he rarely got involved
in the sales side.

I called Patrick into my office the following day.

'I've decided to sell,' I said without any preamble.

'I thought you might have.' He didn't sound too surprised.
'Well, I don't blame you. You did say you wouldn't continue
for many more years. Have you got anyone lined up?'

'Two. They're partners.'

'Have they got any experience of estate agency?'

'No, but one of them's a chartered surveyor. He's worked
for an estate agent for sixteen years. So he knows a bit about it.
They seem bright chaps.'

'Two of them,' Patrick repeated, looking at me with a thoughtful expression. 'That puts me in a weak position.'

'Why?'

'They won't need me.'

'On the contrary,' I said, suddenly feeling guilty about selling and wanting to assure him, 'it's precisely because they *haven't* got estate agency experience that they'll need you. Without me you'll be the only one who knows how to run the actual business side and can deal with the staff.' (I chose not to tell him that Colin had confided his forte was personnel.)

Patrick nodded but I could see he didn't hold out much hope of being retained. He just said: 'We'll see. But don't worry about me – I can always get a job.'

I knew he was right. He was a bright, good-looking chap. He'd never be out of work, though he might not get such a good boss as me, I thought, when he demanded, and always received, a cheeky pay rise every year. Patrick's talent was that he convinced me he was more indispensable than he was. No wonder he was happy with me and was sceptical about two unknown men coming in. They might keep more of an eye on what he was doing. Like toddling off to the gym, for instance.

Two more weeks rolled by. My mother was deteriorating and all she wanted to hear was that these two were definitely going to buy the business.

'They're just getting their finances in place,' I told her, but I was getting anxious and concerned that we'd still heard nothing. Was it ever going to happen?

My mobile went. Alan's voice. Finally. My heart began to thud. I was sure he had some news.

'I've spoken to Colin,' he said.

Yes, yes.

'They're having difficulty getting anyone to lend them the money.'

Bugger. I could see the whole transaction, which as yet wasn't even a transaction, going down the drain.

'They're still confident it's only a matter of time before they get in with the right lender.' He paused, probably waiting for me to say something. I didn't. By now I was fed up to the teeth.

'They've asked if they can have another meeting with you.'

'I don't see the point,' I said flatly.

By then, Alan had met both of them: they'd turned up in his office one day without an appointment.

'I've got a good feeling about them,' he went on, trying desperately to inject some enthusiasm. 'I think they're absolutely genuine and serious, and I'm sure they'll go ahead.'

But the four of us had still not had a meeting. Once again it was just Colin and Nigel and me. They took me out to supper in a very nice restaurant, making a great fuss as to whether it could provide vegetarian food for me. There were beams from them when the waiter said there'd be no problem. I couldn't help thinking what gentlemen they were to be so considerate.

Again, we spoke of personal matters. I asked them how they'd met their wives. They were obviously very proud of these wives, many years younger than themselves, and proud of their families. I thought it was lovely.

'We'd like to take you and your husband out one night for dinner so you can meet our wives,' Nigel said, as we were enjoying our meal. 'It makes sense, as we're all going to be in it together as a "family business".'

'Would you like that?' Colin smiled at me.

'That's a really nice idea,' I said, and I meant it, though privately wondered what we'd all have to talk about if it wasn't the business.

During supper we spoke of everything except what progress they'd made to get the finances.

'We did try to buy another estate agency last year,' Colin suddenly said out of the blue, putting down his knife and fork and watching my expression.

'Oh, yes. Which one?' Obviously I was curious.

He proceeded to tell me the name of the person and the company, which was just down the road from my office.

'Yes, I know them. What happened? It obviously didn't come off.'

'We made an exceptionally generous offer,' said Colin, 'and with a bit of to-ing and fro-ing, we finally agreed. Shook hands. Even signed the initial paperwork.'

'Then the deal fell through,' said Nigel, drawing his brows together. 'And it wasn't our fault. He changed the goalposts at the last minute.'

'I must say, I'm surprised,' I said. 'The owner's never struck me as someone who wouldn't keep to his word. I've always been on friendly terms with him, and he's got a good reputation.'

Colin glanced at Nigel. 'It would have gone through if he hadn't upped the asking price right on the verge of exchange.'

I sucked in my breath. Gosh, was that how a professional person (this particular estate agent was also a surveyor) conducted the sale of a business? I felt quite pleased with myself that I knew how to pull off a successful transaction better than the rivals. Sometimes it takes a woman…

'We pulled out immediately,' Nigel said. 'Sent him packing.'

Nigel's tone was rather cocky, and I must confess I now began to feel quite uncomfortable with this knowledge. They shouldn't be discussing something so private when they hadn't even sealed the purchase of my agency. Possibly not even then. If they were telling me such confidential information, did that mean they would be blabbing to other people about their dealings with me?

Contrary to what the public think, we agents are not at each other's throats. Yes, we're all in competition with one another, often fighting for the same instructions, but it's not unknown for us to ring one another for advice or have a moan about the market. In the main we all get along well together. It was something I would need to point out, though now probably wasn't the right time.

'And it's worked out for the best anyway,' Colin beamed. 'We like your company so much better.'

'Do you really?' I felt a rush of triumph.

'*Really*,' they said in unison.

I was delighted but decided it was prudent to refrain from asking in what way they preferred mine.

After the meal Nigel said, 'We've got something serious to talk to you about.'

I looked at both of them. If I'd been cynical, I'd have thought there was something not quite sincere about their still-smiling faces.

'We're going to have to slightly amend our offer,' Nigel continued.

Oh, yes?

'We can't manage the full 50 per cent up front,' Colin said, looking at Nigel as if for approval.

'But we've already shaken hands on it,' I argued.

'It's not much different,' Colin said. 'But it's going to have to be £400,000 and the other £100,000 in monthly payments over one year. Would you accept that?'

The rules were changing. I hesitated. One of my weaknesses in running a business is that I hate taking ages to make a decision. There are so many dozens of decisions you have to make every single day that it's a great feeling if you can give an answer to one of them immediately. Then you don't have to worry about it any longer. So instead of taking the sensible route and say I would sleep on it and talk to Alan, and because I didn't want to rock the boat, I blurted, 'I suppose I'll have to, so long as we can get things moving.' I felt a little more in the driving seat now they owed me a favour. 'How's it all going regarding the finances?'

'We were promised the finances yesterday.' Nigel looked pleased to be able to tell me some good news for a change. 'They're just waiting for the formalities.'

This cheered me up no end, although the incident regarding their offer to another agent still slightly niggled me. In spite of that we ended the evening on a positive note and more cheek kisses.

Another fortnight crawled by. It was difficult not to lose patience. I didn't want to upset them as I was sure they were trying hard to get the money, but now even Alan sounded worried.

'I'm wondering if they have the wherewithal to pay for this venture,' he said. 'But we'll have to wait and see. There's no one else.'

This was the first time my agent had shown any doubts about their financial situation. And foolishly I didn't ask him if he'd vetted them financially, and whether he was still promoting my business – something I would always do when selling a house. Until that exchange happened I would keep up the viewings. It was so automatic for me; I never thought to confirm Alan was doing the same.

'My accountant was also becoming uneasy.

'From what I can gather, I just don't think they've got the dosh,' he said. 'If I were you I'd ditch them and get somebody else, even if you have to wait another few months.'

James didn't make these kinds of remarks lightly. But how could I wait? My sister and I had been told that my mother only had a matter of weeks to live and I wanted to spend as much time with her as I could.

I also had the sneaking suspicion that selling the business might not be in the best interest of James; he would lose a good client. Yet he'd looked after my financial affairs since I'd started the business seventeen years before and had never steered me in the wrong direction.

I remembered the first time I'd met him. It was my initial free session with an accountant during the Thatcher period when new entrepreneurs had all sorts of help when starting up their businesses. A beautiful aria swept over me as I stepped into his office. An accountant who loved opera? During that first hour James made me laugh. The only other chartered accountant who was funny and witty was my father. I warmed to this new one instantly.

Over almost two decades he'd become a friend, so why would I think for a second that he would give me biased advice? He was too professional for a start. In fact I hoped if it all went through Colin and Nigel would continue to use him.

You can see what sort of a state I was getting myself into. I was becoming suspicious of the wrong people.

Colin rang when I had more or less given up hope of ever hearing from them. He asked if they could meet me yet again. They had some news. I told them my mother was extremely ill but they said it was important and they would take me to a local restaurant for supper. Then if anything happened I could be with my mother in five minutes.

'Would it be all right?' I asked my sister, who was looking after Mum that day. She too was trying to juggle work in my lettings department with spending time with Mum.

'As long as you keep your mobile on,' she said.

The over-lit restaurant was full of happy diners when the three of us walked in. A business acquaintance nodded from the next table as we sat down and I wondered what she would think I was doing out with two men. I always felt on edge when the three of us had a meeting in public in case anyone made assumptions before the deal was done and it got back to the staff.

As usual the boys spoke of other things over the meal. They asked about my mother and showed great concern that she was so ill.

'I remember when my mother died,' Colin said, a sad expression on his usually cheerful face. 'I was so upset.'

'I cried buckets when my mother died,' Nigel said, 'and I'm not embarrassed to admit it.' Tears sprang to his eyes as he recounted what had happened to her.

How nice they are, and how sensitive, I thought. Two really genuine chaps who loved their mothers, and weren't afraid to show it. In those moments I really warmed to them. I didn't stay in that mood for long.

'We're all becoming maudlin,' I told them after a minute or two. 'We should get on to a happier subject.'

'I'm afraid the news isn't too good,' Colin said.

Not again. I couldn't take much more of this.

'We can't get the finance,' admitted Nigel.

'We've been let down by three companies who'd promised us,' Colin added. 'We've come to a dead end.'

I felt them watching me closely. I took a sip of wine, trying not to show my bitter disappointment. There was Mum lying in bed so ill, and I wasn't there giving my sister the much-needed support she deserved. Why couldn't they have told me this over the phone? Or even taken the cowardly route and sent the message through Alan. Irritation bubbled up in my throat and I was about to speak when Colin said, 'There is a way round this.'

'How?' I didn't hold out much hope of any solution of theirs.

'We've got £100,000 between us,' Nigel said, looking at Colin who nodded, 'and if you'd accept that as a down payment we would do the other £900,000 in quarterly payments over the next ten years – the money coming out of the profits of the business.'

Did they think I was completely stupid? Even though I'd had a couple of glasses of wine, this proposal clanged with warning bells that nearly burst my eardrums.

'Sorry, but that's impossible,' I told them, trying to hold back my frustration. I remembered someone at the next table knew me and lowered my voice. 'Ten years is far too long to contemplate and anything could happen in the meantime. The housing market might collapse. We could all be dead.'

I laughed, but inwardly I was angry, not just with them but myself for allowing the two of them to have wasted my evening when I should have been with my mother. And, of course, I'd wasted valuable selling time. Why had I allowed this to carry on in such a pattern? Alan and I had been talking to these two for almost five months. I was aware that we hadn't even signed the Heads of Terms, the non-legal document which sets out all the terms agreed between the two parties which would eventually form part of the contract. Alan didn't seem to think there was any point in signing at the moment as they hadn't got the financial side sorted.

'I think it's the only way moving forward,' Colin said, patting my arm. It was all I could do not to shake him off. 'We've explored every possible avenue and it's the best we can come up with. We still want to buy the business but you've got other things to worry about with your mother, so why don't we finish for the evening and you have a think about it.'

I didn't need time to think. There was no way I would accept this new offer. And I thought both Alan and James would say without question that I must not agree to such a shaky proposal.

Instead (you'll never believe this), I came up with a brilliant idea.

'Why don't you try *my* bank manager?'

They looked doubtful.

'Wouldn't that be a conflict of interests?' Colin said, putting his knife and fork neatly together on his plate.

'I don't think so. Mr Turner, who's my present bank manager, told me last week that a new business manager was taking over and that he was going back to looking after his customers' personal finances.'

'I don't see how that would work,' Nigel said, frowning.

'You can take over the new business manager who doesn't know any of us, and I can keep Mr Turner, as I'll only need someone for my personal account.'

They both leaned towards me over the dining table; I could see they were warming to the idea.

'I've been with them from day one, and they've got all the records showing how much the business is capable of taking and how it's expanded.' I drained my glass. 'They might not want to lose me as a customer and be pleased to finance the deal with the new owners,' I added.

They looked at one another and broke out in smiles.

'D'you know, it might just work,' Nigel said.

'Shall I arrange a meeting?' I grinned, delighted that my idea seemed to be going down so well with them.

'Definitely.' Colin poured out the rest of the wine and we drank a toast to the new bank manager, and that he would recognise a good business deal when he saw one.

I suddenly became tired and looked at my watch, horrified to see it was almost midnight. I was feeling guilty about being so late so I was thankful it had at least ended on a positive note. And I'd eaten well, which was more than poor Anna would've done. I could imagine her only able to snatch a few minutes for some soup and a cup of tea. Mum hadn't eaten anything for the last two days. So after the required cheek kisses and promises to meet again when I'd spoken to my bank manager, I went back to my mother's to find my sister cradling Mum's head.

It was impossible to recognise my mother. Her features were pinched and sickly, and her beautiful blue eyes were closed. Each breath she took was agonising and all I wanted was for her not to go on suffering.

'She's slipping away,' my sister finally whispered.

'Goodbye, Mum,' I said.

Anna got up abruptly and left the room, tears pouring down her face.

Dry-eyed with shock, I held Mum's hand in my own until it went cold.

FOUR

Around the table

It was a few days before I was able to contact the bank
manager and arrange an interview as my time was taken
up by keeping the business running, and offering what help I
could to my sister with Mum's funeral. Somehow I managed to
open another small branch solely for first-time buyers.

But now I was impatient to get a definite date for this
meeting so at the first opportunity I phoned the bank. I was
put through to the man who would have been my next bank
manager, Mr Chakrajevan, and had a brief conversation with
him to explain why I wanted to see him and bring along the
two chaps. He sounded intrigued and said he would be pleased
to meet us all.

I asked the boys if it would be all right if I sat in on the meeting after we'd introduced ourselves.

'Definitely,' said one. 'That's the whole point.'

'We've nothing to hide,' said the other, 'and you being there
will give us some weight. He knows you've been a customer
all these years whereas we've just come in off the street, as far
as he's concerned.'

They must be genuine, I thought, or else they would never
have agreed to my being present. It was almost as though I'd
given them a little test and they'd passed. Any niggles I'd been
feeling about their veracity melted away.

Ten days later the three of us were sitting in Mr Chakrajevan's cramped office. The meeting seemed to go well and when he left the office for a few moments to order us coffee, Colin turned to me with a wink and a 'thumbs up' sign. I nodded and smiled.

At the end of the interview Mr Chakrajevan stood up from behind his desk and looked across at the two men.

'I'm sure I'll be able to help you,' he said. 'The bank knows the history of the company and we know Denise well.' He paused, then said, 'My only concern is that neither of you have estate agency experience. But you say you intend Denise to continue to have an integral role in the business.'

'Oh, yes,' Colin answered. 'Denise is going to play a definite part.'

Mr Chakrajevan looked reassured. 'So leave it with me for a couple of weeks,' he said, 'and I'll see what I can come up with. I do have to put this to my superior but I don't see any problem.'

We all shook hands and left the manager's office in excellent spirits.

Mr Chakrajevan took his time. His couple of weeks turned into a month. It was when I began to think they would never get their loan that Nigel phoned me with the exciting news. They had heard from Mr Chakrajevan, and apart from the final rubber stamp they had the money.

It gave me quite a warm feeling to have sorted out the major problem of their finance. The thought crossed my mind that I was one woman and they were two men, and yet I was the one to have come up with a solution that actually worked. How clever was that?

Veronica, my solicitor, rang to say it was time to have a

meeting around the table with both solicitors and Alan to thrash out the conditions and agreements for the pre-contract meeting. Normally that would first be dealt with in the Heads, she reminded me, but she thought we might as well press on as it was getting close to the end of spring. I agreed as I was conscious of Colin's words that solicitors might be stringing things out.

The Heads of Terms (see point seven of this chapter's checklist) wasn't a legal document – it was simply intentions agreed by both parties. Nor was it absolutely vital. It was the Sale & Purchase contract that counted.

We were getting close to exchanging contracts. Selling a business is not like a residential house sale at this stage; completion usually takes place simultaneously. While this was exciting I realised there was one important thing that hadn't yet taken place.

Nigel, the surveyor, hadn't visited all the offices to inspect the premises. I had mentioned this on numerous occasions and he always brushed me off with some excuse. I'd explained this couldn't take place on a weekday for fear of raising any suspicion among the staff, but any Sunday was fine by me. I had a clear diary for the next few weeks. Still, Nigel hadn't requested a time to do this.

One Sunday I decided to call him. His wife answered and said she would get him.

'Nigel, we'll be exchanging very shortly and time's running out to do the surveys. Can we arrange it for next Sunday?'

'Do you mind, Denise? I'm in the middle of a family barbecue.' He didn't bother to hide his annoyance.

'Nigel—'

'I'll talk to you tomorrow,' he cut in, and put the phone down.

I must say I was a bit taken aback. This was certainly a different side of him which I'd seen no hint of until now. I couldn't understand why he didn't see the necessity of making sure he was happy with the condition of the offices before the exchange. I never took on any new premises without having a full survey. It would have been madness to be responsible for even *one* building for what could be ten, twelve or sometimes even fifteen years without having had a survey. And I was passing on to them *six* different premises of various ages, but all of them old. Since Nigel was a surveyor it wouldn't even cost them anything. It also crossed my mind that if he had such a short fuse he definitely wouldn't go down well with the staff. But then it was Colin who told me personnel was *his* forte, rather than Nigel's. Oh well, if Nigel didn't think it was important enough to do, then I wasn't going to worry about it.

The day of the pre-contract meeting. I looked around the long table. 'They' were up one end and 'we' were down the other. There was my solicitor, Veronica, their solicitor, Mr Fritch, Colin and Nigel looking very smart in their crisp pastel-coloured shirts, serious grey suits, bright ties and their usual matching hankies in their top pockets, and Alan Dorrinne to act as mediator between the two parties. It started off with the smaller issues which we quickly agreed on. Then we got to the first hurdle.

'We've agreed to make quarterly payments of 11 per cent of the turnover,' Mr Fritch began, 'provided the agreed target is reached which will generate the payments. The total amount will be capped at a million pounds.'

My jaw dropped. The solicitor obviously thought he was working in his clients' best interests but didn't he have any idea about sales motivation? That this proposal would actually work *against* Colin and Nigel? In other words, if my payments were capped, where was my incentive to bring in more business once I'd reached the ceiling? But if the sky was the limit and I kept bringing more business in, yes, I would get a modest extra percentage of the turnover but Colin and Nigel would end up with far more. A no-brainer.

'What you're saying is that if the turnover is not enough to trigger a payment I end up with no money that quarter, but if the final turnover at the end of the three-year term is way beyond our forecast I won't have earned a penny extra. No, I'm sorry, you can't have it both ways. It's totally unacceptable. I wouldn't dream of agreeing to it.' I could hear my voice rise.

The atmosphere grew tense. No one spoke. We all looked at one another waiting for the first one to break the silence. It was their solicitor, Mr Fritch.

'My clients and I have discussed the matter and that is what we are offering.'

'Then we have nothing further to discuss.' I scraped back my chair and stood up. Colin and Nigel stared at me in astonishment but I knew I had to score on this point. Why else should I network for them and use my contacts if I didn't have the fun of pushing through the goal of making over that million? The boys didn't appear to have grasped this fundamental concept, which if they were going to have a future in sales they should have understood.

Alan leapt to his feet. 'Let's go into separate rooms and rethink this. I'll act as go-between.' He hustled Veronica and me out of the door.

I was furious. 'The deal's off if the turnover's capped,' I growled. 'I mean it. I'm quite prepared to walk away.'

'Leave it to me.' Alan disappeared and was back in two minutes flat. 'No capping.' The lines on his forehead had visibly relaxed. He'd probably seen his commission about to disappear down the plughole. Colin and Nigel looked equally relieved as I walked back in.

After we resumed Colin went round the table with a jug of iced water, filling up everyone's glass. When he got to me he rolled his eyes and we both grinned. I imagined he was trying to relieve the tension by such a small gesture, wanting to let me know that he was on my side but that these solicitors had their own agenda. (They told me later it had been their solicitor's idea but I had a suspicion they'd readily concurred.)

After more hours of discussion as to how the business would work we came to the question of what amount of time I would put in for them.

'Three days a week to start, then drop down to two days after a few months, and to one after maybe a year,' was my suggestion.

Veronica nodded and took up her pen. She was about to include it in the contract when Colin said, 'Let's just play that one by ear rather than making it formal, don't you think? Keep it flexible.' His voice was casual and his face had a friendly expression as he looked across the table at me. I hesitated. Should I insist? I'd already won several main points in the terms. I didn't want them to think I had to have it all my own way, even on minor points. The three of us got along so well it made sense to play it by ear as Colin suggested.

'Fine by me,' I said.

The meeting came to an end. The solicitors would prepare the Sale & Purchase contract, we would all sign, and then have a final meeting to exchange contracts in about two weeks' time.

In the meantime Colin and Nigel asked me to meet them for yet another supper.

'Just a few minor points to discuss,' Colin said over the phone.

'I thought we'd agreed on everything.'

'There are a couple of things that Nigel and I need to run by you,' Colin said.

'OK,' I sighed.

We met again at my local hotel, and after ordering, Nigel bent down to retrieve a legal pad from his briefcase.

'There are just a few small changes we'd like to make,' he said, scanning his notes.

'Are you talking about altering the Sale & Purchase contract?' I asked, beginning to feel annoyed with the pair of them.

'Only a couple of minor points.' Nigel's tone was reasonable.

He read out two or three which I was sure would not compromise me at all.

'I'll go along with them providing the contract can be altered without any complications or added expense,' I said, 'and providing Veronica's happy.'

Then came the big one.

'To speed things up we want to re-shape the structure of the finances in the contract so the bank manager will allow it to go through ... but there's no need to tell the solicitors as it'll cause even more delay,' Nigel added quickly.

'What do you mean – re-shape?'

'Just a formality,' Nigel said. 'It won't make any difference to your package overall. It's just something Mr Chakrajevan has suggested.'

It sounded a dangerous idea to me. Why would Mr Chakrajevan want to alter anything? Who would benefit from this re-shape? Presumably not me. We'd only just hammered out the Sale & Purchase agreement. No matter how the boys skirted around it I sensed it would affect the structure of my payments.

'This is where I put my foot down,' I said firmly. 'You're talking about a major change in the contract and I'll have to talk to Veronica and ask her advice.'

'No, don't do that,' Nigel said. 'We want to speed up the process, Denise, not spin it out. When that happens the only ones to gain are the solicitors.'

To my inexperienced ear they sounded perfectly plausible, though they didn't seem to be able to explain exactly what this 're-shaping' would entail. I stalled them by saying they would have to put it in writing and then I would think about it. There was no way I was going to make any alterations to the Sale & Purchase contract without talking to my solicitor.

Then they really shook me.

'Did you tell us once that you're intending to change your car?'

'That's right,' I said. 'As soon as contracts are exchanged I'm going to put my order in for a Mini convertible.'

'We're going to buy it for you as a present,' Colin announced.

My jaw dropped. 'Why?'

Shut up, Denise. This sounds good.

'It's a thank-you present,' Colin explained. 'For being so patient and then finding us a lender. We wanted to show our appreciation and this seemed like a good way.'

'It's a fantastic way.' Now I felt rotten that I hadn't fallen in immediately with their request to do this financial 're-shaping'.

Nigel appeared a little more reticent. Though he smiled it didn't quite reach his eyes, and it crossed my mind whether he'd been quite as keen as Colin in offering such a generous gift.

'*And* we're going to have sat-nav installed for you,' Colin beamed.

'I needed sat-nav all those years when I was valuing country houses,' I laughed. 'I can't tell you the number of times I got lost looking for house names in roads with no numbers, down lanes I never knew existed.' I looked at them both. They'd certainly redeemed themselves, and I could hardly believe I had two such lovely buyers.

'Are you absolutely sure?' I said. 'Absolutely,' Colin answered.

There were grins and thank yous, clinking of glasses, and hugs and kisses all round.

The meeting to exchange contracts went on even longer than before. We started at two o'clock. Six hours and a few small nondescript sandwiches later we were still there. Heaven knows why it took so long but after a final read-through with my solicitor to our mutual satisfaction, and the boys with theirs, Veronica announced, 'We are ready to exchange contracts.'

We passed round the various papers, signed over the leases (that had been a whole drawn-out subject in itself), and with the ink still drying, Veronica spoke the magic words: 'We have officially exchanged contracts.'

Colin and Nigel immediately shook hands with one another and then came round the table to kiss me. Everyone was laughing and Veronica poured us all a glass of champagne. I couldn't have felt happier or more clever that I'd actually pulled off the deal.

Checklist:

1. Have your agent thoroughly check the background of the prospective buyers to make sure they are financially secure, and just as importantly, to establish that they are upright and honest characters.

2. Always insist on at least 75 per cent of the offer up front. Try for more if possible. Obviously, 100 per cent is the ideal.

3. It is best to maintain a businesslike relationship with the buyers so you come over as professional and in control. By doing this it is easier when you have to renegotiate or challenge them on any point. Remember the old adage: *Familiarity breeds contempt.*

4. Take professional advice – particularly from those you've trusted over several years or more.

5. It is important that your potential buyers seek their own finance without any help whatsoever from you. Alarm bells should ring if they can't get any financial backing by way of a stable proven record, or if they are reluctant to put their houses up as collateral. If this is the case, instruct your agent to find a new buyer.

6. If your prospective buyers are being turned down by more than two lenders something is seriously wrong. Again, start looking for a new buyer.

7. Make sure the agent keeps the business on the market at least until the Heads of Terms are signed. Even with the

signed Heads there is still no legal commitment until the contracts between you and the other party are exchanged. It will cost your agent more expense and time to advertise your business but that's tough. You're paying the agent a pile of money when the deal goes through.

8. If you are on a 'pay-out to turnover' scheme make sure there is no capping. Solicitors, who are not salespeople, often think they are doing their clients a big favour by saving them money in the future, but it is neither in your buyers' interest nor yours.

9. Do not agree to your buyers requesting a change in the sacred Sale & Purchase contract after it has been signed. If this is altered in *any way* without your solicitor's prior knowledge and approval, it will negate the *whole* of the S & P contract. If you and your buyers want to make a change and your solicitor approves, your solicitor can write it as an addendum to the contract.

10. If you know of any outstanding tasks or things to be discussed and agreed which are still on the 'To Do' list, whether for you or your buyers, make sure you carry everything out *before* the exchange. It will be too late if you leave those things undone until afterwards.

FIVE

The secret's out

'I knew you were up to something,' said Elizabeth when I told her I was selling the business only the day before I told everyone else. 'I hope for your sake they're really nice and will be good to the staff.'

'I think you'll like them,' I said. 'We all get along really well.'

Elizabeth was a wise and loyal friend as well as my personal assistant. She'd worked closely with me for sixteen years. Her family call her a witch because her judgement of people is uncannily accurate. It wouldn't have been risky to have told her, I realised, as she was totally discreet and ready to retire anyway. Her job wasn't at stake to influence her opinion.

'I'm really pleased for you. You've worked hard and you deserve it. But two inexperienced men…' she trailed off, sounding doubtful.

'Nigel is a chartered surveyor,' I assured her, 'and he's worked in an estate agency for sixteen years. And Colin ran a business about the same size as mine.'

'When do I meet them?'

'Tomorrow,' I promised. 'When I introduce them to the staff.'

'Does that mean you've already signed the contracts?' Again, that hurt look that I hadn't taken her into my confidence.

'Yes, we have,' I said. 'But don't worry – I know you'll like them.'

She removed her glasses and looked at me. 'Well, if I don't, it will be too late.' Her words rang out in the upstairs office we shared.

When you're an employer you feel responsible for your employees – and I had fifty to look after. Their continuing welfare was important to me but equally I hoped they would give Colin and Nigel a chance.

I called an Extraordinary Meeting at a favourite Victorian venue way out in the country where I'd booked a private room. Instantly the company grapevine went into operation overtime, the various offices buzzing about what the news might be.

After we had all gathered I told them my plans. They were fantastic. They said they didn't blame me; most of them knew my age (I'm not sure how) and had thought it might not be too long before I retired. But of course they were anxious about who would be taking over.

I reassured them the buyers were two of the nicest chaps, perfectly capable of running the business, that Patrick would still be there as general manager, and for the first year at least I'd be around.

'I'm selling the whole business,' I explained, 'and you're all under TUPE (see point one on checklist) which is your legal protection. That means the buyers are responsible for you; none of you can be let go, and all your time working for me counts as far as holidays … and any possible redundancies,' (there were one or two nervous glances) 'but we don't expect any at all,' I continued hurriedly, 'and all the terms and conditions we've individually agreed remain in place. So there is absolutely nothing for you all to worry about.'

Most of them seemed relieved, though I noticed a few

sceptical faces. I decided it was time to bring out the boys, like rabbits from a hat. I went out to one of the back rooms and gestured for them to come in. Everyone's head swivelled. Colin and Nigel were smiling and cheerful without any sign of arrogance – striking just the right note. I felt quite proud of them. After introducing them I asked if they would each tell us a bit about their background, which they did. Several people asked questions which Colin and Nigel answered easily and openly.

We then had a glass of wine and the boys circulated among the staff, chatting and laughing. I loved seeing everyone looking relaxed and friendly. The bit I'd dreaded was over.

The three of us lingered awhile after everyone left.

'Well, that went absolutely fine,' I remarked.

'They seem a good crowd,' Colin commented.

'They're a super bunch, though some of them can be quite challenging,' I laughed. 'One of the criteria necessary to be a negotiator, I'm afraid. You have to get involved with them on a personal level – show you care.'

'Fine,' Colin said with a serious expression. 'I told you, I love getting involved with people. It's one of the things I'm really good at.'

'Patrick will be pleased.' I picked up my handbag. 'He hates dealing with their problems. He'll have plenty to do showing you how everything operates and keeping up with the salaries and spreadsheets.'

We walked to the car park together.

'We've got something to show *you*,' Nigel said, waving his hand at a couple of shiny sleek cars. 'Look what we've bought.' He pointed to two brand new Jaguars, one maroon, the other black. My mouth dropped open. I couldn't believe it.

'Yours?'

They nodded, grinning.

'Are you sure you should be spending all this money so early on?' I said. 'They must have cost a fortune.'

'Don't worry – they won't have any effect on the business,' Colin assured me. 'We used our own money. And because we bought two at the same time we got a great discount.'

What could I say? They were going to buy *me* a new car so why shouldn't *they* both have one? But a kernel of doubt set in. They were spending a huge sum of money before they'd even taken over. My own accountant had made me wait three years before he allowed me to buy a new car so this expenditure so early in the game seemed bizarre. Were they going to be spendthrifts? I brushed the idea away. They were two mature men who must know what they were doing. Really, I told myself, it was nothing to do with me what they did with their private money.

My last staff conference was set for the end of May, where of course Colin and Nigel would feature prominently. They had already prepared their presentation but wouldn't show it to me. They said they wanted me to enjoy it as well as the staff. I was a little uncomfortable with this idea. I'd been caught out before at a couple of get-togethers with the staff when I hadn't known in advance what the presenter's content and delivery would turn out to be. But if the boys couldn't do a presentation without my input it would be a pretty poor show, I reasoned. I decided to let them go ahead.

Colin and Nigel sat at the head table next to one another, then me, then Elizabeth, and next to her, Daphne, my book-keeper. By the time everyone had gathered we had over fifty people. If I hadn't known them all so well it would have looked quite scary and I wondered if the boys were thinking: *My God, whatever have we taken on?* But they seemed undaunted.

As usual I asked each manager to stand up and give a report on how their office was performing. Then Patrick went through the figures for the company and who had made top office, who had sold the most financial leads, and so on. Several bottles of champagne were distributed and there were happy faces amid the clapping. Finally it was the turn of Colin and Nigel.

Colin spoke first.

'I'm really delighted to be here and thank all of you for your support in the new company. Nigel will now give you his presentation which I'm sure you'll all enjoy. Nigel?' And Colin waved his arm in a dramatic flourish.

There was a round of polite applause. I was on edge not knowing exactly what they were going to say, but couldn't help feeling quietly smug that I had brought about this sale. I was still going to be very much involved in the business. I was looking forward to giving any advice, introducing them to my special contacts, etc., but most of all not having to go in on a daily basis. Of course I was very aware I was on an earn-out payment scheme, which was not ideal, but the contract gave me certain rights such as access to the monthly figures and management accounts, and I would do everything I could to ensure that Colin and Nigel retained our highly prized service and reputation.

Another phase of my life was about to begin.

All these thoughts rushed through my head as Nigel proceeded to give a slide show of how he thought the business would operate, how he and Colin would fit in, Patrick's continuing important role (thank goodness), and then the spotlight was turned on me. Up came a cartoon of a woman sitting on the beach under a palm tree, all alone except for her computer, barricaded by a tumble of books. For some reason my stomach turned over and I forced myself to unclench my hands.

'And there's your old boss,' Nigel indicated the distant character with his battery-charged pointer. 'Gone off travelling … doing her own thing … writing her book … enjoying her retirement. Leaving the business to *us* to run.' He smiled but it didn't quite reach his eyes and I sensed Elizabeth giving me anxious sidelong glances.

That last remark unnerved me too, especially the emphasis on 'us'. It sounded as though Nigel was making a strong point directed at me but coating it in an innocuous way. Any whisper of doubt I'd had about their competence to run an estate agency this size flared up, and at that moment I seriously wondered if I'd done the right thing. To calm myself I decided I must be behaving like a 'singleton' (as Bridget Jones would call it) about to give up her freedom. All would be fine when I'd actually done the deed. Walked down the aisle, so to speak. I wasn't so attached to my business I couldn't let go. And, of course, I trusted the boys to do a great job. My freedom was beyond any price. And so I continued to enjoy the conference and laughed along with everyone else at the lonely little figure on the deserted beach.

Checklist:

1. Look into TUPE (Transfer of Undertakings [Protection of Employment] Regulations 2006) with an employment specialist/solicitor. If you sell and the staff are under TUPE you will have protected them from any alterations to their contracts by the new buyers.

2. If you have anyone who works in your business or who owns a similar one, who is truly trustworthy and sensible, and who holds no vested interest in the outcome, use their expertise and talk over your plans. It can be tremendously helpful to have another opinion from someone you have confidence in, who knows the business and understands what you are trying to achieve.

3. Have your antennae up for any doubts, niggles or worries about your buyers *at all times*. Don't wait until it's too late and you've exchanged contracts. Pride doesn't come into it. CALL A HALT IN THE PROCEEDINGS.

SIX

The takeover

I bumped into the boys on their first day. I was on my own in a small Italian café near the head office in the late afternoon having a cup of tea and feeling quite peculiar. Where was the euphoria I'd expected? Why was I suddenly so worried? I swallowed my tea and finished my scone without really tasting it. Gesturing for the waiter to bring the bill I looked up at the sound of the café door opening. To my surprise Colin and Nigel strode in, beaming from ear to ear when they spotted me. They ordered their coffee and came and sat with me.

'We had a feeling you might be here,' they said.

'So how did your first day go?' I was dying of curiosity.

'Splendid,' Colin said, swigging a mouthful of coffee. 'Didn't it, Nigel?' He looked at his new partner as though needing confirmation. I'd often noticed him doing this – wanting approval or for Nigel to confirm what he'd said. It seemed a bit wimpy to me.

'We've had a busy day,' Nigel said. 'It's going to take a while but we'll get there. We're ready for anything.'

'Really?' I was impressed, knowing the huge undertaking. But did *they* realise? No way could I have taken on such a large company. It was only that I'd 'grown up' with it that I'd just about been able to cope. For Colin and Nigel it was like taking on a family of eight rowdy teenagers, rather than the babies I'd nurtured and brought to maturity. But then there were two of them and they seemed very confident.

'Well, you know where I am if you need any advice,' I told them. 'You will keep me updated, won't you, on what's going on?'

'Yes, of course. We'll always keep you in the loop,' Colin assured me.

I brushed away the thought of what a silly expression that was. He was full of jargon, but I reckoned it was just his manner. It made him quite endearing, I told myself.

'So when are you going on holiday?' Nigel asked.

'You can't wait to get me out of your hair,' I teased. I'd already mentioned I would leave them in peace for the first three weeks so they could settle in and get to know Patrick and the rest of the staff.

They grinned.

'When I come back we'll sort out the days I'll be working for you,' I said.

They glanced at one another again, smiled at me and nodded.

Everything was going to work out beautifully.

I needed to see the boys again before I went on holiday so one morning I popped into head office. One of the girls told me I'd find them at a certain café down the High Street.

'They meet there every morning for breakfast,' she told me.

I don't blame them, I thought. Having a regular meeting first thing was sensible, so why not combine it with breakfast?

It was a warm early summer morning. I practically skipped along, so excited with the sale I'd achieved and my freedom which was finally within my grasp. Going into the office once or twice a week, maybe not even for the whole day, would feel more like pleasure than work.

I glanced in the window of the estate agency the boys had

almost bought, feeling a little sorry for the owner who hadn't pulled it off and was still having to work, even though he was older than me.

It wasn't difficult to spot Colin and Nigel and Patrick sitting outside enjoying the sun, their table filled with cups of coffee and croissants. They looked as though they were on holiday in France. I couldn't see any sign of a structured meeting – not a notebook or pen in sight.

They all looked up and smiled, pulling out a chair for me to join them. I declined the offer of coffee as I just wanted to run through a few things and disappear.

'Enjoy your day, then,' I said as I put the list back in my bag. 'I'm off to do some shopping for my holiday.'

I left them to it and dived into my favourite department store. This was the life.

I was ecstatic. I was to have a fortnight's holiday in Germany; actually, it was in Bavaria, at a sanatorium called Tannerhof, where I worked in 1973 as a vegetarian cook. It had been an extraordinary year and I was determined to write a book about my experiences. I'd started it, but very slowly because of the business. Now I was virtually free of the responsibility I could make some real progress. It was also going to be my sixtieth birthday, which I wasn't particularly looking forward to, but illogically it wouldn't feel so bad spending it in a foreign country. And Tannerhof was celebrating its centenary a few days later. I knew they'd put on a magnificent show.

Perfect timing.

I came back from Germany happy and refreshed, even though unfortunately a year older. My first job was to phone the boys suggesting we meet soon to catch up. They sounded very upbeat and asked about my holiday, but all I was interested in was how the business was going. We arranged to meet the following day but to my disappointment Sharon, Colin's sister-in-law who acted as their personal secretary, emailed me early that morning to say that Colin wasn't able to make it after all. Nigel, though, was happy to attend. I wanted to see both of them so we deferred until the following week.

We arranged to meet in my old office on the second floor. I almost didn't recognise it. The harsh masculine look was straight out of a 1980s office brochure. The room had been completely refitted with new filing cabinets, computers, telephones, visitors' chairs and a pair of leather-topped desks, each with its own executive chair. Worryingly, there was no sign of any work being done. No files, no paperwork, nothing. Just clear desks. Maybe they were incredibly tidy workers. The office refit must have cost a fortune. My God, these two really knew how to spend. But when I looked more closely I could tell it was far from top quality.

'What do you think?' Colin beamed, looking around as though he were a proud new father.

'Very nice,' I said.

'You don't like it, do you?' Nigel said frowning.

'Well, my lovely second-hand desks were solid oak and like new,' I couldn't help saying. 'They were larger, for one thing, and they would have lasted a lot longer than these veneered ones will.' A rolling of eyes passed between the two men which I pretended not to notice. I pressed on. 'What happened to them?'

'Oh, someone came and took them away,' Colin said.

What a shocking waste.

'Well, you've certainly put your own stamp on the place,' I concurred, and they both smiled and nodded, presuming, I'm sure, that I was paying them a grand compliment.

'Oh, there's some post for you.' Colin ambled over to the new fake cherrywood bookcase (which was empty), and retrieved a couple of envelopes from a metal filing tray perched on the top. He handed them to me with a flourish, as though to show me how efficiently the room acted as an office. Had they already forgotten how well it had served Elizabeth and me for the last decade?

I glanced down at the envelopes. They were both marked 'Personal'.

'I was going to ask you about that.' I examined the post-marks. 'People will gradually stop sending personal stuff to me at the office, but will you let me know if any more comes and when I can collect it?'

'You're welcome to come to our office whenever you like,' Colin said.

'But if you're not here?'

'Just come upstairs – it's your old office anyway – and we'll leave anything in a filing tray marked with your name.'

Nigel hadn't said anything at this point. I saw his mouth harden. Suddenly, I realised he was not happy with Colin's invitation.

'I don't like to do that if you're not around,' I said, quite sincerely. After all, if the situation were reversed I wouldn't want them coming into *my* office any time they pleased.

'You're perfectly welcome to do so,' Colin smiled. 'I mean it.'

But I never once entered their office unless they invited me, which was rare. It wouldn't have felt right.

I was keen to show Colin and Nigel my new flashy gold Mini convertible they'd so generously said they would pay for. They'd recently requested that for tax purposes I buy it in my name on monthly instalments, and they would reimburse me each month. I wasn't quite so happy with this arrangement, knowing they could stop the payments at any time if they so wished. After all, the gift of the car was not down anywhere in writing. Then I mentally shook myself. It was a present and I had no reason to think they wouldn't keep their word.

I checked my bank statement which was waiting for me on my return from holiday and was delighted to see that the first three up-front payments had already gone into my account together with the total amount of the sat-nav bill.

Before I sold I'd belonged to a business network club and one member had given me some fantastic leads. The first one was a house of £1.5 million and there was a spin-off from the sellers who recommended my company to two of their friends. They ended up both giving me their houses, one valued at £600,000 and the other at well over a million. We sold all three properties and the commission of around £45,000 had gone straight to Colin and Nigel. On reflection it was bad timing on my part. I should have delayed the exchange on that alone. It did cross my mind but where do you draw the line? I'd wanted to produce healthy figures, and show that we sold the up-market properties as well.

Anyway, I emailed Colin and asked if I could take the manager of the branch that had sold them, together with the lovely lady club member who had introduced these clients, out to supper. And would he reimburse me? Without hesitating he said 'yes'. The bill came to a modest £120. I invoiced him. He ignored it. I reminded him. I never got reimbursed. Was this going to be a pattern? No, of course not. He was busy with coming to grips with the new business, that was all, and must have overlooked it.

Checklist:

1. Even if you've received your full payment up front for your business it's sensible to be around during the first months of your buyers taking over, so try not to book holidays in this period. Definitely don't go abroad. There are bound to be questions which only you can answer. If you're on an earn-out payment scheme it is *imperative* you stay close by.

2. Keep the contact flowing. Meetings are vital, even if the circumstances aren't perfect; for example, if one of your buyers can't attend. Insist that the agreed date be kept anyway.

3. Of course you want to be thought of as being a nice person but that does not give the new owners the right to take advantage of you. You must at all times act in a professional manner. Be prepared to iron out even a small matter if it is important to you.

SEVEN

Serious doubts

Two years before I sold I had instructions from a developer who we'd never worked with before to sell his block of eight apartments. Emma, the manager of our new homes department, and I were thrilled. We'd worked hard to show him we were the right agents for his development when there were as many as thirty others in town. We'd made suggestions to the floor plans, advised on the fittings and had worked out a full marketing regime. Timothy, the developer, would have nothing to worry about so far as presenting and selling them.

It was a real feather in our cap as we would have a huge board outside with the company's name emblazoned on it. Also, it was bound to bring in other business, i.e. from buyers who wanted to go the next step up, or downsize, and I would have the chance of selling their own homes if they lived locally. It had taken all this time for planning permission to come through and the build to complete. This was a great shame as once again I was handing Colin and Nigel what would be a most lucrative development without their having lifted a finger towards it.

But don't be greedy, I told myself. This is all part of the sale price.

Timothy was visibly nervous when I explained I was in the process of selling the business. The launch of the flats was to be the weekend after I returned from Germany.

'Don't worry at all,' I told him. 'I'll be there on both launch weekends, and Anna as well.'

My sister, Anna, had designed and dressed the show flat and Timothy was thrilled with the results.

'Just promise you won't let me down,' he said more than once. 'I would never have instructed two unknown men who were inexperienced.' He looked at me. 'I gave you the business because of your reputation. So far you've done a superb job, plus there's the fact we get on so well.'

'I'm going to finish the job I started,' I said reassuringly, 'but you'll like Colin and Nigel. They're really keen to be involved.'

The boys had asked their wives to provide the refreshments for the open day and the women had done a fantastic job. They'd prepared enough food to provide around fifty hungry browsers with a full plate of canapés. There was a selection of sparkling wine, soft drinks and mineral water.

The three of us set everything out on the kitchen worktops of the show flat, and I could tell Colin and Nigel were very proud of their young wives' endeavours. I thought how nice that was.

Anna arrived to do the final fussing with the show flat. Eventually, she was satisfied. It looked stunning, and I began to feel the buzz of adrenalin, imagining myself arranging the sale of a couple of the apartments on this first day.

My sister left rather abruptly, which surprised me as she was scheduled for the whole day. She was good at showing buyers the merits of a property and overcoming any of their reservations. As she'd been so involved in the presentation of these individual apartments she knew all their various drawbacks and assets. I was relying on her to help me as Colin and Nigel simply didn't have the experience. She'd been unusually quiet that morning but I just thought it was because she was concentrating on the job in hand.

People started to arrive. Immediately, I swung into negotiator mode and never knew what transpired with Anna until later that evening when she came over for supper.

'I'm not at all keen on your buyers,' she said. 'They were extremely rude to me, especially that Nigel.'

'Whatever about?' My heart plummeted. I couldn't bear to think any of the girls were spoken to rudely, let alone my sister.

'He rang me yesterday and said he didn't need me at the opening. That the show apartment was ready and that I was no longer employed by Denise Barnes. He said for me not to turn up today.'

I felt sick. My sister does not exaggerate. Besides, I had my own story to tell her.

'What did you say?' I asked her, dreading to hear.

'I said, "The show apartment isn't quite finished and I'll be there early in the morning to make the final adjustments before anyone arrives." Nigel didn't answer, but I'd have gone anyway. Timothy wanted me there.'

'Good for you. I'm glad you told him.'

'If they treat all the staff like that they'll have a walk-out,' Anna said.

The staff *were* the business. It was they who would work hard to make sure the business not only survived but was successful. What on earth possessed Nigel? How dare he? My temper flared.

'I'm going to tackle them about it. I'm not having you spoken to like that.'

'Please don't mention it,' my sister said. 'Maybe they're still finding their feet and aren't as good at handling people as they made out. But I shan't go next weekend. I'm sorry, Den, but I've got a bad feeling about them.'

Terrible doubts were now assailing me. I'd had a pretty awful day myself with Nigel. I told Anna what he'd said at the very start of the day.

People had just begun to arrive. I'd started talking to a couple who were the first ones to look over the apartments and had now wandered outside to get a feel of the surroundings. Nigel had walked up. To my astonishment he completely ignored me.

'*I'll* take over from now on.' His tone was challenging as he practically stood in front of me to get close to the couple. '*I've* bought the business so you'll be dealing with *me* and my partner from now on. It's nothing to do with Denise Barnes any longer.'

My jaw hung open. Nigel, who had after all worked in an estate agency for many years, didn't have a clue as to how you should treat people. Almost worse, he had no inkling as to how you go about selling a property. And I'd sold my precious business to him.

I knew this would take a while before his words sank in and how it would affect our future relationship, but for now I needed to concentrate on the weekend. Timothy must not have any hint as to what was unfolding.

The couple looked bemused, realising they were unwittingly the cause of some kind of internal argument. Desperate to hide my embarrassment I gathered my wits and calmly told them to follow me inside. I made the excuse I wanted to give them more information about maintenance costs and so forth. We left Nigel standing, furious.

In spite of Nigel's rudeness the day was a success and we had a firm offer on one apartment from a couple who were renting and strong interest on another two, with valuations on their houses booked in. Not bad at all. But the result showed how ignorant Colin and Nigel were.

'I thought all the apartments would be taken up this week-end,' Nigel said.

'All eight?' I looked at the two of them in amazement. 'You've got to be joking. Estate agents actually have to work hard to tie up sales. It doesn't all fall into your lap, whatever the public think.'

But I could tell by their expressions they thought the launch was a disappointment.

At the closing of the day I managed to report to Timothy when Colin and Nigel were busy clearing up the food and drinks.

'That's excellent news,' he said. 'Better than I expected.' He looked at me anxiously from his lofty height. 'Denise, I do want you to continue to handle the site and monitor the sales.'

You have no idea how much trouble that might cause, I thought.

'I've got nothing against the new owners,' he continued, 'but this site is too important to me to leave with anyone who hasn't got the experience.'

I promised to do so, thanking God he hadn't heard Nigel's crass remarks.

When I relayed all of this to Anna she nodded as though she wasn't surprised.

'I just wish you'd have let me meet them before you signed contracts,' she said. 'I would have begged you not to sell to them. I can't understand how you didn't pick up on their vibes. They looked to me like a pair of incompetent fly-by-nights, and not at all who you'd want to take over your business.'

Anna is often right in her judgement of people but she does

tend not to give anyone a second chance if they slip up just the once. So again I tried to push my own worries to one side. I didn't dare voice them but she knows me better than anyone. I didn't have to say anything. She knew I was regretting my decision to sell to those two.

I called a meeting early Monday morning with Colin and Nigel.

'Timothy wants me to handle the development,' I began, heart sinking as they frowned. Colin was flicking the top of his biro in out, in out. Nigel's features suddenly weren't so pleasant. 'Don't take it personally,' I went on. 'You have to put yourself in his shoes. He doesn't know you, and he and I have had a business relationship for two years now to get to this point.'

Still silence.

'He insinuated that if you don't allow me to be in charge of the site he may well disinstruct us. And that would be awful.'

That would get them, if anything would, I thought. But I was in for another shock.

'You will *not* be involved,' Nigel said coolly. 'Emma will take over.'

'What?' I had to stop myself from shrieking. 'Are you mad? It's eight units totalling forty grand's worth of commission, *and* the second-hand properties you'd get as a result. Emma can't be available every day including weekends to take people over. But I can, even at short notice.'

'We'll take that chance.'

'But if we lose the business we'd have to take the board down. It's such a great advertisement for the company.' I was gabbling now. 'You really can't afford to upset him.'

'Emma, as I said, will be taking over,' Nigel repeated, leaving pauses between the last four words. 'You will not be required.'

'Colin,' I turned to him, baffled, 'do you agree with this? Are you willing to risk the possibility that Tim might give his development to another agent?'

'Nigel's in charge of new homes,' Colin said, not looking me in the eye and flicking the top of his biro. 'It's his decision.'

'And it's *our* business,' Nigel warned.

It was becoming very clear they thought they knew best.

There was nothing I could do. They were right. In our contract it was completely their business. Unfortunately, I hadn't taken proper notice of my accountant when he told me he'd suggested to Veronica that the transaction should be under a shares system equal to the monies outstanding. Veronica had mentioned this but warned me it might jeopardise the sale. And that was the last thing I'd wanted to do.

I finally admitted to myself that I'd made the worst mistake of my life by selling my business to these two clowns. They had no idea or concern as to how to treat prospective clients who would be putting money in their pockets, which meant they wouldn't care about the staff either. And the more I thought of my sister, the more upset I became.

Checklist:

1. Listen carefully to your accountant's advice. They have probably known you and your business for years and want the best deal for you. Regarding the remuneration and its structure, the accountant is in a much better position to advise you than the solicitor acting for you in the sale who you may never have met before now.

2. If you don't receive all the money up front, make sure you keep shares in the business to the same value as your buyer still owes you. Then when a payment is made you can relinquish the appropriate number of shares. In other words, every time they make you a payment, your buyers will be closer to owning the whole company, and you will still maintain some control over the business until you are fully paid.

3. I haven't mentioned this before, but although your accountant can usually advise you on tax affairs when running the business, it pays to speak to a tax specialist when selling, as there are numerous ways to avoid (not evade) or reduce some of those frightening demands.

EIGHT

The honeymoon is over

Shortly after the fiasco with the eight new apartments I received a curt email from Nigel saying they would not be holding weekly meetings with me, that it was a waste of time, and that nothing fruitful could come of them. He also warned me not to get into direct contact with Timothy, the developer. Everything had to go through him. He didn't even mention Colin so presumably he, Nigel, was taking over any new build.

In his hands I was sure the development was doomed. And I doubted very much they would ever be instructed on another one.

By now it was November and I hadn't received the first quarterly instalment. The second one was actually due. I began to feel uneasy, especially as I'd already reminded them in two emails but hadn't had an answer. I hated having to ask. I'm not embarrassed about money in the slightest (I'd lived in the US too long) but I didn't feel I should have to beg for my money. Money that was rightfully mine. It was somehow demeaning.

Gritting my teeth I picked up the phone. Colin answered. After the preliminaries I said, 'Colin, when am I going to have my payment for the first quarter? The second quarter is due now so the first one's very late.'

There was such a long silence I thought we'd been cut off. But there was no give-away dialling tone. And I hadn't heard the receiver being put down.

Alarm bells jangled. Maybe he was going to ask me if I'd
accept the payment in two lots. Well, I wouldn't concede as I
could tell by the monthly figures that the business was healthy
and making a good profit. I heard him clear his throat.

'Denise, you've reneged on the dilapidations.'

Something in my brain clicked. I took a deep breath. 'What
are you talking about?'

'You haven't left the offices in good condition.'

'There's nothing wrong with the offices,' I said, trying not
to rise to his accusation. 'I've always kept them up. They—'

'Don't worry,' Colin interrupted smoothly. 'We'll work
things out. We need to itemise everything and send you a report.'

'You're making a serious allegation, Colin,' I said, 'so I'd prefer
to discuss it in person … as soon as possible. Also,' I continued,
'I haven't received the last three payments on the Mini.'

'Don't worry,' Colin repeated. 'We know about it. We're in
the process of setting up a direct debit.' He rang off.

I put the receiver down, feeling sick to my stomach.

After some persuasion Colin and Nigel agreed to meet me at
one of the hotels in town. When I arrived I saw Patrick was
with them. It was beginning to irritate me that I couldn't have
a talk with my buyers without him there but they'd obviously
invited him. It wouldn't have been quite so bad if he'd been his
normal friendly self to me, but he said very little and when he
did speak it was completely in support of his current employ-
ers. I had the childish thought that it was three against one.

After all the small talk, which only increased my irritation,
they came to the crux of the meeting.

'We haven't paid you because of the dilapidations,' Nigel
said, drawing a sheaf of papers from his briefcase. 'I've done
a full report on all the offices and I'm afraid there's a lot to be

desired. You've failed on Fire Regulations, Health & Safety, and the general maintenance of all the buildings. We were told that Fire Regulations could close the company down in ninety days if they saw how little protection the buildings have. In other words, you're in breach of the warranties.'

I was shocked. Not because I believed there was a grain of truth in Nigel's declaration, but because I now realised they'd planned this all along to stall my payments. What a fool I was. Colin didn't say a word. Nor did Patrick. I suppose they thought this was Nigel's speciality. He handed me the wad of papers.

'Is this my copy?' I asked Nigel.

'Yes,' he said. 'And I think when you read it you'll understand the reason why we haven't paid you. The amount we're claiming, which we have to spend to make good, approximates £100,000.'

'Really? A nice convenient round number,' I commented, my tone thick with sarcasm. 'Who's carried out this survey?'

'Who do you think?' Nigel smirked. 'I have, of course.'

'And you didn't think it might be a conflict of interests?' By this time I didn't attempt to hide my anger. 'You didn't do any surveys on the premises before you signed the contract even though I asked you several times. Whenever I've signed a new lease do you think I'd do it without getting a survey done to make sure the building was in good order? When I'm responsible for years? So why didn't *you*?'

Nigel didn't answer that. He merely said: 'Just read it through.'

'We don't expect you to pay for *all* of it, but we want to offset the payments to meet some of these costs.' Colin threw me an apologetic smile.

'If you took the trouble to read your contract,' I said through

clenched teeth, 'you'll see that if you have any claims against
the warranties you have to wait until you've paid me *in full*.
You can't take it upon yourselves to deduct what you see fit
and ignore paying me. I'm disgusted with your tactics. I'll be
putting this in my solicitor's hands.'

This was our first row. To my mind it put a serious blight on
our relationship. Later, when I thought about it, I wondered if
my expectations were too high. Maybe when such large sums
of money are exchanging hands it's impossible for everything
to go smoothly without a few blips.

'We'll get a cheque off to you straight away for £25,000
against the first instalment to be going on with until we sort
this out,' Colin said in what was meant to be a soothing tone.
But it only inflamed me more that my money was hanging in
the balance.

Swallowing my fury I said coldly, 'I'll be most grateful.'

When I arrived home, I made a pot of coffee and opened the
pack of papers that Colin and Nigel had warned made horri-
fying reading. Nigel's report was about forty pages long and
divided into office headings. He'd used the company's headed
notepaper. I was pleased about this as at least it would prove
to any solicitor that there was a powerful conflict of interests.
The report was so exaggerated and inaccurate it would have
been almost laughable if my position hadn't become so serious.
None of the buildings, Nigel claimed, were in any fit state for
their purpose and some were apparently too dangerous for the
staff to be working in.

It's a wonder they hadn't closed all the offices down immediately, I thought, tossing the papers on top of the filing tray.

I had meticulously gone through all the offices before I
employed the business agent so I wouldn't have to be faced
with a sudden deluge of repairs and redecorations. As I've

mentioned, most of the offices were in older premises but were perfectly sound, and with one exception the landlords were responsible for any major works on their buildings. I was only responsible for decorating, minor repairs and the windows. If Colin and Nigel had any concerns regarding structural repairs they should go direct to that particular landlord.

I picked up the Health & Safety report. It was several pages long but it wasn't from the council as I would have expected. Instead, it was a private individual I'd never heard of. This person hadn't used headed paper, nor had they dated or signed it.

I didn't think it would hold up in any court.

That evening I wrote in my diary: *The honeymoon is over. There is a side to them that is most unpleasant. I got very angry but they wouldn't budge. We have had to call a truce. I could at any moment have burst into tears. It wasn't much fun having three men who were all against me, but I hope I managed to hold my own.*

I hadn't seen Colin and Nigel (as you can imagine, I'd long since stopped calling them 'the boys') for over a month but I'd decided to try not to nag or complain and make the next meeting positive. We went through a few things on my long list. Then they socked it to me.

'We're changing the logo.' Nigel's face was smug.

'*What?*'

'Yes, we're bringing it more up to date. It's old-fashioned.'

'I can't believe this,' I shook my head. 'Everyone knows the logo.'

Silence.

'You are going to keep the cat?' I asked.

'Oh, yes.'

Phew. That was a relief. Everyone knew the sign of the black cat. Even dogs have been known to jump up at the boards and bark, their owners having to drag them away.

Seriously, the cat was crucial. When the pubs had quiz games and everyone had to guess the various logos they always knew the black cat trademark. So you can see how important it was to me for the business. Sometimes we'd be asked, 'Is that the Black Cat agency?' and of course we would say 'yes' – we didn't care what they called us so long as they found us.

Heart in mouth, I wondered what this new logo would look like.

'Have you got a proof for me to look at?' I asked them.

'No, but don't worry – you'll approve,' Nigel said in a tone that told me the subject was closed. I wasn't going to be fobbed off. The logo was too important.

'I'd really like to see a proof.'

They looked at each other. Then Colin said quietly: 'Denise, you *must* understand, this is *our* business and we really must be allowed to get on with it as we see fit.'

Driving home, eyes stinging, all I could think of was how different this had turned out to be. It seemed their true person-alities were really showing themselves and I didn't like it one little bit. How had they managed to keep up the charm all those months before we signed contracts? How could I have been so stupid? So full of my own importance, thinking how clever I'd been to pull off the sale of my precious business.

It was December and I heard through the grapevine that the staff were having a huge treat but it was to be a secret. During our chats before completion Colin had said I would be invited to the Managers' Meetings (I never was once) and would I be the star at the Christmas party?

'You'd enjoy that, wouldn't you?' Colin had given me a charming smile. 'And we would love to have you.'

'Sounds fun,' I'd said.

You've guessed it – I didn't receive an invitation. But on thinking about it, we'd gone beyond the stage of get-togethers at jolly Christmas parties so I tried hard not to let it get to me.

There was one small consolation. The new logo wasn't as bad as I'd feared. They'd added what they thought was some clever shaded colouring which to my mind was a complete waste of money. But at least they hadn't changed the name. It must have cost them thousands to recreate the change on the brochures, stationery, fascias, A-boards, advertising and so on. They obviously thought this was more important than paying their debts. I didn't bother to tell them that shaded logos went out ten years ago.

Checklist:

1. Make sure your buyers have had an official survey carried out on all your leased premises *before* your solicitor allows you to exchange contracts. Ensure you receive a full report from them in writing and it is 'signed off' as being satisfactory. Alternatively, instruct your own surveyor, send your buyers a copy of the report and make sure they sign it. If you neglect this vital step your buyers could claim you have breached the warranties and withhold any further payment(s). This could happen even though your contract clearly states that the purchasers must wait until they've actually finished paying you the full amount for the business before they can make any claim.

2. Your solicitor should make it part of the contract that the buyers are not allowed to change your logo or name unless you have been paid in full. I cannot stress how important this is; it should be an integral part of the contract if you are on a payment schedule. It's the only way your good name, and therefore repeat business or recommended new business, will continue. Any name change will alert the public that you are no longer at the helm, or indeed, that it is a completely different company with different staff, and they will look around at the competition.

NINE

Changing solicitors

No surprise that my promised cheque amounting to £25,000 for a halfway payment didn't materialise.

I sent a long and detailed email to Veronica, my solicitor, telling her all the latest developments. Getting no reply after a couple of days, I phoned.

'I'm afraid Veronica's on maternity leave,' the receptionist said. 'Her cases are being dealt with by Mr Hill-Morgan.'

So why hadn't he picked up my email?

'Did you receive my email where I outlined all the points?' I asked Mr Hill-Morgan after I'd introduced myself.

He didn't seem to know what I was talking about.

'I'd better send it to you again,' I said, frustrated that we couldn't continue until he'd acquainted himself with my file. 'Can you phone me when you've read it and gone over the contract?'

He said he would.

The landlord of one of our town offices rang me that afternoon. He sounded annoyed.

'You've transferred the lease under Licence rather than Assignment,' he began.

I'd had great difficulty working out the various procedures of transferring the leases, especially as this should all have been carried out before completion of the transaction, not weeks later. This was due to Colin and Nigel being very lax on signing their part of the Assignments. I had constantly reminded them to get the paperwork signed and sent back to my solicitor as it was holding up the last part of the completion. Of course I didn't mention it was leaving me in a vulnerable position, on which this landlord didn't hesitate to enlighten me.

'If your buyers don't come up with the signed documentation in seven days I shall forfeit the lease,' he warned, 'so you'd better speak to them pronto.'

It didn't take much for me to work out that he could then come in and change the locks.

'I'll get on to it right away,' I promised.

I decided to email Colin about the lease as I wanted to put it in writing. I told him the landlord had threatened to forfeit the lease and his next step would be to change the locks. A few days later Colin sent back the necessary paperwork, signed by him and Nigel, and there was only the matter of my signature before I was able to pass it on to my solicitor.

Mr Hill-Morgan eventually rang me back, but said it was complicated and asked whether I could go over and see him in person. It took two train rides and a taxi to get to his office.

'I've had a look at the contract,' he said, 'but there's not much you can do unless you want to sue them, which would be very costly.'

What else is new?

'Surely the contract was drawn up to protect me from things such as the buyers deciding how and when they will pay me.'

'Maybe you should be patient,' he said, to my astonishment. 'The first year will be difficult for them financially, especially as you've had all the money from the exchanges.' His tone smacked of what a greedy woman I'd been – and obviously still was.

'That was the deal,' I said through gritted teeth. 'The exchanges were nothing to do with the buyers. I've left them with a half-a-million-pound pipeline, and there's more than enough money in the bank, but they still refuse to honour the payments.'

The solicitor simply shrugged. 'Let's see how things go,' he advised.

My solicitor's bill had been £22,000, plus VAT. I think I deserved more than a shrug.

I decided the only way to inject some energy into my predicament was to change solicitors. A professional friend recommended a Mark Billinghurst who apparently 'took no prisoners'. Just the kind of person I needed. He worked for a company on the coast – not very convenient but far enough away to maintain privacy.

Mr Billinghurst greeted me warmly, told me to call him Mark, and offered me a seat in his shabby Dickensian office. He'd been briefed by my friend and was delighted to help.

'I like a challenge,' he told me, and I didn't doubt it for a moment. He looked quite a bruiser with his shaved head and stocky build, clad in cream trousers held up with bright red braces. His face, however, appeared crestfallen as he began to read through my contract.

'The trouble is,' he paused, looking up over the top of his glasses and tapping the pages, 'this contract is full of loopholes. There's no penalty for not paying you except for a bit of extra interest. And if you're not receiving your payments the increased interest is meaningless. You say you have the monthly figures and they've reached their target?'

'Yes,' I nodded. 'And beyond.'

'And they're now two payments behind?'

'Getting on for three now, and I've had nothing at all.'

'I'm afraid the contract is worded so you will have to sue on every payment, whether they're late, or miss one. It *should* read that if they're late, say, for two payments,' he clicked the edges of the contract with his thumb and forefinger, 'then they will have to either pay you the whole amount or the business reverts to you – with immediate effect. That's how I tied down buyers into a recent contract for my client. It works like a dream. Your way, it will cost you to sue them every single time. And if this becomes a habit you're in for spending a great deal of money to try and retrieve what's owing to you.'

My heart sank.

'I'm afraid my hands are tied,' he added glumly, 'but we'll write them a strong letter reminding them of their obligations and that in accordance with the contract we want the first payment made within seven days, and the second payment two weeks later.'

Mark worked his way through the documents and paid particular attention to the warranties, which is where, I explained, the problem seemed to lie. He agreed with me that the new owners couldn't just deduct what they had arbitrarily decided were the cost of the dilapidations. Any claims, according to the warranties in the contract, *had* to be made at the end of the three-year payment period. Colin and Nigel were using the so-called dilapidations as a handy excuse for not making the payments.

'They've also stopped making the monthly payments on my car,' I told him.

'Have you got anything in writing that the car was included?'

'No. It was never in the contract. Just something they promised me they would do.'

'Well, a verbal contract is just as binding, though a little more difficult to prove.'

'So what do you think should be the next step?'

'How about us getting around the table with their solicitor and the two of them?' he suggested. 'Perhaps we can sort this out there and then. If we can, it will be a lot quicker ... and a lot less expensive for all of you.'

I thought it a good idea and he made contact with their solicitor, Mr Fritch.

A few days later Belinda, who worked on Saturdays, told me everyone had been warned in no uncertain terms that they were not allowed to talk to me, and then she showed me the following email:

> This is to confirm that Denise Barnes is no longer a consultant for this company, nor does she have any involvement at all. If she comes into your office she is to be treated with respect but on no account are you or any members of your team to give her any information whatsoever about the business. If any members of staff contravene this order there will be serious consequences.

What on earth were they trying to hide? What did they think I would do? What did they think their staff were going to tell me?

Though it was signed by the branch manager, I could tell Colin had composed it and given the order to the managers to circulate it. The tone was his, especially the mealy-mouthed bit about treating me with respect. I wished he would take note of his own words.

Later, Colin denied all knowledge of the email even though

I'd actually seen it, but I couldn't tell him as I didn't want to make things awkward for Belinda. She'd been quite brave to show me the email in the first place as she was a foster mother and desperately needed her Saturday job.

But I never took to this particular manager, Kevin, though here I only had myself to blame. Patrick and I had originally interviewed him although he had no experience in estate agency. All he had was a year working in a lettings office, which is an entirely different business. Patrick, however, had persuaded me to take him on as there really wasn't anyone else suitable who'd applied. Against my own rule of never hiring someone because there was no one better, we employed him. He started at the same time Colin and Nigel took over, and from day one Kevin thought he knew it all.

Occasionally, I stopped at the one office I owned, just to say hello, but the girls were always incredibly nervous that I had even stepped over the threshold. Megan, the secretary, who had worked for me for several years, would put her finger to her lips and incline her head towards the adjoining office where Kevin sat with his back to the front display window on the High Street, apparently playing computer games.

Then in a louder than normal voice, in her thick Scottish accent, she'd say, 'Hello, Denise. How lovely to see you.'

That would bring Kevin straight out of his private corner. He'd walk through the archway and take over any conversation even though I would pointedly ignore him.

If he decided to snitch on the staff, or indeed, me, he'd pick up the phone with no hesitation and report to Colin. I'd already warned Colin and Patrick that Kevin was bad news but of course they took no notice. They wouldn't hear a word against him. He was obviously now one of them – one of the boys. There was no point in talking to Nigel. We were barely communicating. I didn't want to compromise the girls in any way so I stopped going in. But every single time I drove past it was as though someone was sticking a knife in me. I'd grip the wheel and swallow hard, forcing myself to stare straight ahead.

Despite ongoing warnings to have nothing to do with me, several of the girls kept in touch regularly, telling me how Colin in particular treated them: one moment all smiles and smarm, and the next he'd have them on the carpet in front of their team for something petty. He rarely checked he'd even got the right member of staff. This was from someone who'd said his forte was personnel.

Checklist:

1. Make sure the contract contains a strong enough incentive for your buyers to pay you. A hike in the interest rate is no threat as it's such a small amount in the grand scheme of things.

2. The sanction for two late payments should enforce the buyers to pay the whole purchase price within fourteen days or the business reverts to you. You should avoid having to sue separately for each late payment.

3. Always check any professionals, even if they come highly recommended, before instructing them. The business agent is only one source for professional recommendations. Talk to, and get quotes from, at least one other in the same profession so you can make a comparison.

4. Swanky solicitors' offices (or any other professionals') by no means signify quality and service. It's the track record of the individual that counts. They might have a shabby office in some backwater but deliver brilliant results.

5. Always check any paperwork that is given to you as 'evidence' is written on headed notepaper (phone the company if you are at all suspicious), and obviously check it's dated and signed.

6. Leases are a separate issue. Make sure they are all ready to be assigned simultaneously on exchange of contracts of the business.

TEN

Bust-up

I received an email from Sharon to ask if I would attend a meeting. I phoned her.

'Anything in particular?' I said, wondering if there was anything I needed to bring with me.

'Not that I know of,' she said too quickly.

By her tone I knew she was perfectly aware what the meeting was about. It was highly unusual that *they* were calling a meeting. It was always me, and then they would often cry off at the last minute. This must be something important. What were they going to throw at me now?

I arrived at the hotel early (to give the impression of being in control, even though I feared I wouldn't be), and looked for a table where we might have a modicum of privacy. A few minutes later Colin and, of course, Patrick sauntered in. Why did Patrick always have to be there? Couldn't they do anything on their own? This time I would definitely say something. But first I asked, 'Where's Nigel?'

'He won't be coming. Let's order tea and I'll explain.'

They refused to enlighten me until the tea tray came. Then Colin dropped the bombshell.

'Nigel and I have had a bust-up. He's no longer a partner.'

'You're joking.'

'I'm perfectly serious.'

'But the contract says you can't change the partnership. And you have to have two partners.' They were running true to form now, I realised, not bothering to consult me on anything – big or small.

'There *will* be two partners.'

I looked at Patrick, who was silent. Over my dead body, I thought.

'Patrick?' I couldn't help throwing Colin a disbelieving look. I wouldn't allow myself to look at Patrick again.

'No, my wife, Sandra.'

'But she knows nothing about the business.'

'She'll be in name only.'

I didn't like the sound of that. There would only be one working partner. Colin only had six months behind him, in which time he'd shown little interest in estate agency or the staff who worked hard to keep it going – not to mention the ridiculous decisions he'd either made or concurred with. You'll know by now that I didn't rate him capable enough. But Colin was very upbeat and said it would be seamless. He said that Nigel had done so little no one would ever notice the difference.

'What happened? I thought you two were bosom buddies,' I said.

'We are … were,' Colin hurriedly added. 'And this is going to have a devastating effect on our wives with their business, as well as the end of a fifteen-year friendship.'

I couldn't have cared less about the wives' business or Colin and Nigel's fifteen-year friendship. 'So tell me—' I began.

'Nigel was supposed to set up a surveyors' department.' Colin snapped the top of his biro in out, in out.

'That was supposed to be part of the plan,' I said. 'It was his way of bringing in some business. But so far I haven't seen any results.'

'Nor have I.' Colin sounded genuinely annoyed. 'He kept going to London on the excuse that he was interviewing prospective surveyors. Whether he saw anyone or not, I don't know. But I do know that he had a good time … expensive lunches and such … and put the bills in to the company for reimbursement. I told him more than once he'd have to start doing some surveys himself if he didn't soon get a department going, but nothing changed. I'm better off without him.'

I was stunned. They'd obviously not bought the business on a whim and they'd known one another for a long time. But somehow it didn't ring quite true though I couldn't begin to work out why. All I knew was that it was a *fait accompli*.

Patrick, who had been silent up until now, spoke up.

'I shall obviously be even more involved,' he said, a pleasant expression arranged on his regular features.

'I don't see how that particularly helps me,' I snapped, gratified he looked surprised at my tone. 'I sold the business to two *so-called* professionals,' I paused and looked directly at Colin, 'who promised to do everything in their power to keep the business on track, promote it, and even expand it. So far, nothing of the kind has happened. It's been a shambles right from the beginning.'

I know this kind of observation doesn't go down well with men who particularly hate being criticised by women, but by now I was so frustrated with their incompetence and their way of barring me from any of their decisions I couldn't stop myself. Talk about Colin's promises to always keep me 'in the loop'…

And I hadn't got over my annoyance that Patrick was at the meeting. This should have been a private discussion. The news had come as a complete surprise and I wanted to talk to Colin on my own. Also, I wanted to bring up the subject of still not receiving any payments. Nor had I had any further payments on the Mini. And I didn't want to do any of this in front of one of my ex-employees.

Colin excused himself to go to the Men's and I took the opportunity of saying I needed to go to the Ladies'. We left Patrick sitting there. I quickly touched up my lipstick and waited for Colin to come out.

'Colin, can I have a word before we go back into the restaurant?'

'Sure.' His pasted-on smile did nothing to win me over.

'I'm really not at all happy you insist upon bringing Patrick to every meeting. They're private and he's just an employee. I *have* asked you not to before. Another reason is that Patrick seems to have turned against me, though I don't understand why. He's barely polite any more and quite frankly I don't want him present.'

'Yes, I have to agree that Patrick does appear to have changed towards you.' Colin slid a sideways glance at me, then looked quickly away.

It crossed my mind that Colin might be out to make trouble between Patrick and me. But for what reason? I dismissed the thought and told myself I was becoming paranoid.

'And while we have a minute on our own, can I remind you about my payments. I've had nothing and the third one is due in a fortnight. That's nine months without any payment. You promised me at least a cheque for £25,000 right away after our last meeting but I still haven't had anything.'

'I'll get it organised,' he assured me. 'You'll have it within a few days.'

More procrastination but I always believed him – he was so convincing. (I know you're thinking you can't believe how gullible I was, but you'd have to be there to see the way he operated.) I decided if one of them had to go I would rather it be Nigel – he could be so rude.

'And the Mini,' I reminded him.

'Would you write an invoice for the amount each month and put that it's a consultancy fee?' he said. I raised an eyebrow. 'It would be tax beneficial.'

'I couldn't do that,' I answered. 'I always ran the business with scrupulous honesty so nothing could ever come back and bite me.'

He rolled his eyes but said no more. It would have been pointless to tell him what had once happened to me.

When I first started up in 1988, a seller whose house we'd just successfully sold had come into the office carrying a small leather suitcase. (You can see I'm going back a long time – it was before those handy little wheels.) He snapped open the case to reveal rows of bundles of notes.

'Your commission,' he said with a flourish. 'But without the VAT.'

My commission was around £3,000, plus, of course, VAT.

He began emptying the bundles out on my desk, some of which fell to the floor. The girls' eyes almost popped out of their heads.

'I run this business absolutely straight,' I told him firmly. 'And I'm not going to take cash even if you give me the extra for the VAT.'

He gathered it all up and went out in a huff, saying I could wait for my cheque.

And that was before we had any warnings on money laundering.

Back to Colin. We joined Patrick at the table and Colin continued his story.

'Nigel was lazy and hadn't brought a penny into the business. He'd originally said his surveys would bring in £100,000 a year which would go into the pot. I'd incorporated it into the calculations when we first decided to buy the business.'

'So had I,' I told him. 'The turnover triggers my payments. So we're both losers.'

'Well, it caused a major row and I've had to pay him off.'

'How did you have the money to pay him off?' I asked suspiciously, privately thinking it was funny he could pay Nigel off but he couldn't pay *me*.

'Oh, it was only £2,500,' Colin said airily.

'Pardon?'

'Yes, that's all Nigel put into the business – £2,500.'

'Only £2,500? But if I'd known that, I wouldn't have sold the business to you,' I said, raising my voice, not caring how livid I sounded. 'It's crazy for a partner to put in so little. No wonder he didn't worry about turnovers and expenses if he hadn't invested a proper amount of money to begin with. He hadn't risked anything. I can't believe it.' My brain was whirling. Then I remembered something Nigel had told me. 'He said he was going to re-mortgage his house so he could put in his share.'

'He doesn't own his house. He rents it from my mother.'

I looked at him in amazement. Nigel had had no financial commitment whatsoever in the business.

'You told me once you *both* owned your houses. When we were about to complete.'

Colin averted his eyes.

'And it didn't worry you that he was such a financially weak business partner?' I went on. 'That he had so little at risk it might as well have been nothing?'

'It didn't worry me because he convinced me he was going

to add such value by his surveys. But I'm happier now he's gone. Patrick and I can get on with the job and not have the frustration of Nigel doing nothing but swan around in London pretending to put a team of surveyors in place.'

I was speechless.

Then Colin said, 'Oh, just to let you know, another agency has been given the new apartments as joint agents.'

'I'm very sorry to hear that,' I said, 'but not surprised. I could see it coming. But it's a real shame as the commission will be halved. I think Timothy was very worried when I was taken off the case. Nigel didn't give him any confidence that we were the right agency for the business. He was far too arrogant.'

'Just as well he's gone, then.'

And that was more or less the end of the meeting.

I phoned Alan Dorrinne.

'I'm ringing to tell you that Colin and Nigel have had a bust-up,' and I described the meeting.

'I'm really surprised,' Alan said. 'They'd always said how they'd wanted to go into business together for years, and yours was the perfect opportunity.'

'The perfect opportunity not to pay me,' I said, bitterly. 'Besides, I didn't think there could be any alteration in the partnership under the contract.'

'You'd have to check that with your solicitor.'

Without thinking I posed the question I'd been wanting to ask for ages. 'Alan, did you vet Colin and Nigel to see what their financial circumstances were?'

'Why do you ask?'

'Because Nigel only put in what amounts to a packet of crisps,' I said. 'All of £2,500. And he had no collateral at all. Apparently, he rents his house from Colin's mother. Even though Colin told me once they both owned their own houses. I can't believe anything any more from those two. If I'd known what I know now I would never have sold to them. It's just a joke.'

'I didn't know he'd put down such a small deposit,' Alan admitted, 'but I'm sure the business will continue to be successful with or without Nigel.'

But he hadn't answered my question about whether or not he had financially vetted Colin and Nigel.

'It *is* successful, according to the statistics I get every month,' I told Alan. 'But that's not down to them. It's down to the staff. The money's rolling in but I still haven't been paid, and the third one's due.'

Months later, when I thought about Alan's response I was cross with myself to think I'd let him persuade me that Colin would be fine to run the business on his own. Then I thought, why should Alan exert himself? I'd already paid him his £42,000. All right, that included VAT, but he still had £35,000 clear for his company where he was one of the directors. He obviously thought his responsibilities were over.

I told James, my accountant, what had happened. He did a quick check on Nigel and found out that he was running a separate residential surveyor's business and turning over a fair sum of money annually. He had neglected to put this into my turnover figures as stated in the contract. Surely Colin must have known this.

'You should take this up with your solicitor,' James said.

Checklist:

1. Always insist that any private meeting you have with your buyers during negotiations, or when they become the new owners, is between you and them. And your solicitor if it warrants it. Under no circumstances should an employee be there, as even if your buyers ask your permission and you agree, issues may arise that you would not want an employee to be privy to.

2. This is another reminder for you to make sure the business agent has checked your buyers' financial status. It could make all the difference when deciding whether to sell to them or not. An accountant can also make some easy checks on your behalf.

3. If you have a concern and you discuss it with the appropriate person, make sure at the end of the conversation you know how to take it further. Don't be fobbed off. Talk to another professional, preferably your solicitor, while it's still current. It's no good complaining later as by then it's bound to be too late.

ELEVEN

Not fit for purpose

Colin was still using the dilapidations as an excuse not to pay me. I decided it was time to respond once and for all to the question of the dilapidations, or 'delapidations' as Nigel had spelt it in his report. It wasn't going to go away. So Mark, my new solicitor, suggested I employ my own surveyor and he recommended someone he'd worked with on many occasions. Also, he'd heard from Mr Fritch that Colin and Nigel were willing to sit around the table and thrash out the so-called warranty problems.

The meeting was to be held at the usual hotel. The receptionist guided Mark and me to a small separate room we'd hired. 'They're already here,' she whispered.

'I bet Nigel won't be,' I said to Mark, who wore a serious navy striped suit. The red braces were nowhere in sight.

'He ought to be. He's a personal guarantor, so just because he's no longer a partner he's still fully liable.' Mark opened the door and ushered me in front.

Sitting opposite were Colin and Patrick. No Nigel, as I'd predicted. Mr Fritch got up to introduce himself and shake hands with us.

'Before we start I would like to ask why Patrick is here.'

The words dropped from my lips. As you are now very aware, I was none too pleased with Patrick. His whole demeanour had changed towards me. We used to have a joke and a laugh but now I'd become the enemy. He'd gone over to the other side — I'm sure believing that was where his croissants were buttered.

'Because I invited him.' Colin's voice was smooth. 'Do you have any objections?'

'Yes, I do,' I snapped. 'Patrick is an employee and I don't want him privy to my personal affairs. He was not invited and I would like him to leave. This minute.'

There was a moment's silence. Patrick sat there looking uncomfortable.

'In fact,' I seethed, 'I refuse to carry on with this meeting if Patrick doesn't go.'

To my annoyance Mark intervened. 'I don't think it matters, Denise. Let's just get started.'

Mr Fritch nodded, looking relieved. I pressed my lips together to stop myself from arguing.

'Let's begin with the dilapidations,' Mark began, 'as they seem to be causing the main problem.'

Mr Fritch riffled through his papers. 'Unfortunately, your client left the premises of the various offices in a very poor state, and my clients are having to spend huge sums to get them in a presentable and safe condition for the staff.'

Before I could open my mouth to protest, Mark stepped in.

'May I enquire first where Mr Zennerming is? He should be at this meeting.'

'He's no longer a partner,' Mr Fritch confirmed.

'But he's Ms Barnes's personal guarantor, exactly as is Mr Dixtrow.'

'He didn't see it was necessary to attend,' Mr Fritch said.

'Well, he is certainly liable,' Mark argued, 'so I would have thought he'd want to listen to what he is still responsible for, particularly as I understand it was he who carried out the report on the various offices. However…' Mark proceeded to explain that Colin and Nigel couldn't make a claim until the money was paid, which led us on to the issue of my lack of payments. 'It also states in the contract,' Mark went on, 'that to my client's knowledge the offices were left in serviceable condition.'

'She knew full well they were not fit for purpose,' said Mr Fritch. 'So the clause is null and void.'

It was unnerving listening to a professional solicitor spouting his clients' trumped-up accusations.

'If they're not fit for purpose,' I interrupted, 'and Nigel's mentioned to me that one or two are actually *dangerous,* why are the staff still working there? I'd have thought you would have told them to evacuate the building.'

Colin looked at Patrick. Neither of them answered. In the silence Colin clicked his pen in and out.

'The contract clearly states that if there is any contesting of the warranties it cannot be offset against the payments and can only be dealt with at the end of the payment schedule,' Mark persisted.

'May I say something before anyone makes any comment?' I said. 'I was selling to two *supposedly* intelligent men.' I glared at Colin. 'And Nigel told me at the onset he was a *chartered surveyor*. Is that true?'

'Yes, he is,' said Colin, speaking for the first time since saying he'd invited Patrick to the meeting.

'If that's so, wouldn't you think he would have checked all the offices *before* you exchanged contracts?'

'You wouldn't let us,' Colin said, his eyes shifting away from mine.

My mouth hung open. Then I let rip.

'Excuse me,' I raised my voice. I couldn't help it. 'Weeks before we exchanged I asked Nigel several times to survey the offices. I said I couldn't let him carry out any inspections on a weekday as I didn't want the staff to know, but I said any Sunday I'd be pleased to spend the whole day on it and he could go round all of them. He said he would. I even phoned him at home and he was extremely annoyed. He said he was in the middle of a family barbecue and didn't want to be disturbed. And put the phone down on me. How *dare* you say I wouldn't allow him in?'

Colin said nothing – just twirled his pen round and round on the table. I noticed he always fiddled with his pen when he was in the wrong or telling one of his lies. I was becoming expert on his body language.

'It seems to me this was all carefully planned so you could present my client with a spurious list of repairs *after* you'd actually bought the business,' said Mark. 'Very convenient.'

'And as far as saying you've had to spend a load of money on the properties, I have it on the best authority you've spent *nothing*.' I half rose from my chair. 'But *if* you are telling the truth – which I very much doubt – you might like to let me see the invoices for all these tens of thousands of pounds that you have allegedly spent.'

'That would be a great help,' Mark continued. 'And I've told Ms Barnes to get her own survey done of all the premises. When she does, we'll review it. Let's move on. So why have you stopped her car payments?'

It was a casual question. I couldn't wait to hear the reply. I looked at Colin; now he was flicking the top of his pen. It was beginning to get on my nerves.

'The car wasn't part of the contract,' he said, after a moment's hesitation.

'It was a verbal contract,' from my solicitor.

'The car was offered on a past agreement,' Colin said, warming to his lie. 'We've changed several things since then and the car doesn't now come into it.'

'Are you saying that the car was only offered *before* the exchange of contracts, and when certain things changed, you and Ms Barnes agreed she wouldn't have the car after all?'

'Yes.'

'Then why has she received the first three payments *since* you took over the business? In other words, *after* the completion date, which presumably was under the current contract.'

Colin flushed but declined to answer. He glanced at Patrick, whose expression was glum. The clicking pen started up again and I wanted to scream.

'You know we agreed on nothing of the sort,' I said, trying to look Colin in the eye, but he was obviously more fascinated with his pen and empty notepad. 'You're telling another outright lie. The Mini was a gift from both of you to me, and now you've left me stuck with all the payments for the next three years. I should have known when you wanted me to put the car in my name for, as you said, *tax purposes*.'

I know I'd already planned to buy myself a new car but that wasn't the point. They had reneged on their promise. All that toasting with wine when they announced they were giving me a car as a thank-you. How generous I'd thought they were. They must have laughed themselves sick at the way I fell for everything.

(Weeks later one of the managers said that Colin had told everyone at a meeting he'd paid me in full for the business and had even bought me a brand new Mini convertible.)

Colin didn't answer. I began to wonder why he was there at all. The meeting went on for a bit and we broke into two groups at one point when Mark considered it was getting too heated and we needed a five-minute break. When we came back Mark had a list of proposals he and I had agreed, along the lines of the previous discussion. Mr Fritch glanced at the list, then read them out.

1. Ms Barnes will get the offices surveyed by a chartered surveyor and report back.

2. The two outstanding quarterly payments to be made in seven days together with all interest accumulated. If it does not materialise, Ms Barnes will sue.

3. Ms Barnes will not press for the car payments but will continue to make them herself. (This one I argued with Mark but he said it was too minor to worry about.)

There were a few other points which we all agreed to and then Mark declared the meeting closed.

In response to the above meeting, in January 2006 I received my first instalment payment, five months overdue. In April I received the second payment, in July the third, and then nothing. Dates were just ignored though Sharon, the PA, continued to send me the statistics so I could see they were still making a good profit and the turnover was higher than anticipated.

I decided to go back to Mark who promptly sent Colin and Nigel a threat that we would sue. Two weeks later I received the fourth payment. Interest which had racked up to more than £2,000 was ignored. Mark managed to recover the fifth payment and then it all went quiet.

Checklist:

1. Sometimes a round-the-table meeting with both lots of solicitors can resolve issues, provided everyone wants to get things sorted with the least trouble, expense and stress. It is certainly a lot cheaper and more convenient than going to court. In the event of a dispute I would urge you to at least try this method first.

2. Don't rely on anything verbal that has been agreed. Always have it recorded in writing.

3. Be highly suspicious of any expensive presents. These might easily prove to be bribes. Remember these old adages: *If something sounds too good to be true, then it is*, and *There's no such thing as a free lunch*. (Or a free car.)

TWELVE

Disastrous logo change

I'm not sure who decided it was time for yet another logo change now that Nigel was off the scene. The last change had definitely been his idea, so I don't think Colin would have thought it necessary to change it again as the first one wasn't more than a year old. He must have been persuaded it was the right time to make a clean sweep.

I was incredulous and very upset when I saw the new logo. It was bright red and white, cheap-looking like most of the corporates, with just my initials: DB Estates. What kind of estates? Country house estates? (They'd be lucky.) Council-housing estates? One estate agent actually tried to spread the rumour that DB Estates only dealt with the lower end of the market, particularly specialising in ex-council houses. I almost couldn't blame the agent. It was such a silly name and what did the DB part mean? Why did they hate the name when that was what they'd bought? My name was synonymous with my reputation and I felt sure instructions would start to diminish.

Once again they would have spent thousands of pounds to make these changes which in the end I was sure would *lose* them money. It's probably impossible to change your logo without it costing at least £20,000, and that would be working on a strict budget. They'd done it twice in the space of fifteen months. I did it once in seventeen years. I decided they either just loved spending or their egos were so big they couldn't bear to see my name anywhere.

Any business consultant would tell them they were crazy.

One of the girls told me she'd seen Patrick carrying a mock-up of the new board into the office a few weeks before, and when she challenged him as to why Colin had changed the name, Patrick apparently said, 'We need to disassociate ourselves from Denise as quickly as possible.'

As if I were some criminal.

When she asked him why, he didn't answer.

My forecast came true. The negotiators were finding it more and more difficult to gain instructions. Prospective sellers thought the company no longer had anything to do with me and went to other agents. This was way before the start of the downturn of the housing market.

People began to stop me in the street and ask why on earth I'd changed the name. I'd explain that I'd sold the business and it was nothing to do with me.

'But that was surely what they bought – your name,' they'd all say, disbelievingly.

I tried to get a meeting with Colin but he ignored my requests. I was worried that this would have such a dire effect on the business that there wouldn't be enough income to generate the rest of my seven payments, not that there was any hint that I'd be receiving any more money, but now it seemed there'd be no chance whatsoever.

Every time I saw one of the new For Sale boards or the re-painted fascias on the various offices I felt as though someone had kicked me in the stomach. I would feel it churn and I'd try to drive past as quickly as possible. It sounds ridiculous writing this but it was true. I wasn't getting paid. I wasn't included in anything. I had little contact with Colin. No wonder he'd said at the exchange of contracts meeting that we should just play it by ear how much work I'd be doing each week. As it was, I was more or less banned from even going into the offices.

I felt completely alienated.

I received the report from the independent surveyor on the various office premises. He could barely come up with more than £6,000 worth of works which he thought could possibly have been carried out by me prior to the sale but, in his opinion, this was still questionable. His bill to me was also £6,000. I sighed. All these thousands of pounds going down a bottomless pit. We sent the report to Colin's solicitor who reiterated why his client wasn't going to be paying me any more money – because I was in breach of the contract and warranties. So my surveyor's report and Mark's insistence at the meeting that I be paid regularly and on time hadn't made a scrap of difference.

'The only thing now is to threaten to take them to court,' said Mark. 'Your sixth payment is … surprise, surprise … overdue, and maybe we can combine the two issues.'

I told him to go ahead.

'It will cost in the region of £50,000,' he warned. That did rather stop me in my tracks.

'How can it be so much?'

'We'll have to have a barrister,' he explained. 'And the case could easily take a week … possibly longer. As your solicitor I must warn you to think about it carefully and coolly. Don't let emotion get in the way.' He looked across the desk at me. 'But if you do decide to go ahead, there's nothing I'd like better than nailing these bastards,' he added gleefully.

I couldn't believe it. My little business warranting a week or more in court to sort out something that was blatantly clear to me – they'd received more than enough money to trigger my payments but they refused to hand over the rest of my share.

I resolved to give the matter some serious thought.

Checklist:

1. Always weigh up the risk when your solicitor warns you of how much a court case will cost. And even if you win there is no guarantee that you will get your money. Furthermore, it will be very stressful for you to appear in court day after day, answering questions, particularly from the defendant's barrister who is there to trip you up.

2. The approximate cost quoted could end up being doubled if the judge deems it to be less than straightforward and it takes longer.

3. Be sure to have it written in the contract how long you are remaining in the business, how much time you will give, what contribution you intend to make, and finally what salary you will earn. This is probably best calculated on a daily rate. It works both ways. The buyers need your help and you need to make sure they are competent to run it. The only time you can break this rule is if you are paid *all* the money up front.

THIRTEEN

Strange meeting

James rang me one day and asked me if I would speak to Colin. Apparently, Colin had told him some 'startling' information and he, Colin, would like to tell me about it as well.

'Why doesn't he speak to me direct?'

'He knows you don't trust him and wanted me to approach you first. I think you should go and see him. From what he says, it sounds genuine.'

Colin doesn't know the meaning of the word.

I was reluctant to go as by now I thoroughly disliked the man. But curiosity got the better of me. So I telephoned him. Colin was as charming as could be. When he was like this I often used to think it was *me* – that *I* was the one who was paranoid, unreasonable, and misinterpreting their intentions. But I was finally beginning to learn a few lessons and was now on my guard. The whole saga was really getting me into quite a state and more than one friend was worried I would end up having a nervous breakdown. Anyway, we made an arrangement for me to go to his office the following day.

The girls all looked up in surprise when I came in and several of them got up from their desks and gave me a hug and a kiss. 'Hello, stranger,' they said, but it was a weird atmosphere, as though my presence made them feel uneasy. I remembered how

lovely the atmosphere used to be when I would pop downstairs
and have a chat and a laugh with them. Now you could sense a
kind of unseen malevolent presence. They were on edge in case
Colin should appear at any moment and remonstrate with them.

Nicola, the manager, who was still seated at her desk, immediately stretched out her arm for the phone as I made my way
to the back of the office to the stairs. 'Denise is here,' she said,
her tone urgent, as though she was worried she would get into
trouble if I simply by-passed her. 'Shall I send her up?'

She nodded to me to go up to his office.

'Welcome, welcome.'

Colin appeared at the top of the second flight of stairs, his
smile broad, waving his arms for me to go up. He even, can
you believe, wanted to kiss me and looked disappointed when
I turned my head abruptly and asked if we could get down
to business.

I let him talk.

'Sorry, I'm so sorry ... how badly we've treated you,
Denise,' he began, eyebrows pulled together, feigning contri-
tion. Really, he should have gone into acting. 'All of us,' he
went on. 'Nigel, Patrick ... and even me. But I realise now that
it was Patrick who turned me against you. So I became suspicious of you, thinking you were going to cause me trouble.'

Charming.

His comments about Patrick, whether or not true, were
disloyal, considering Patrick was, I would have thought, his
most valuable employee.

Colin repeated himself again and again, mindlessly, until
I thought I would go mad. He must have said he was sorry
fifty times, and that is truly no exaggeration. After the first few
times I just switched off. Finally I could take it no longer and
asked: 'Can we cut to why you invited me here?'

He looked a little taken aback that I hadn't burst into tears of gratitude on account of his barrage of apologies. But he soon pulled round.

'I've mentioned Patrick because you may not know I've fired him.' He watched me closely to see how I was taking this.

This took me completely by surprise. Whatever my personal feelings were towards Patrick he was good at his job and I didn't see how Colin could do without him. I'd always thought they were two buddies together, especially now Nigel wasn't part of the equation.

'Really? What happened?' I was genuinely curious to know why.

Colin leaned back in his chair and tapped his pen on the desk, looking rather smug that he'd got my attention.

'It's difficult to know where to start,' he pretended to muse, and so increase the drama of his following words, 'but there's a huge amount of money missing. It was supposed to be a VAT payment of about £70,000 and the VAT inspector came round recently to pick up the cheque. Instead of asking to see me he went and spoke to Nicola and told her the bill hadn't been paid. You can imagine how that went round the office. I'd authorised for the cheque to be sent to them so it was all very embarrassing.'

There was a long silence while Colin waited for me to put two and two together. It was too far-fetched to be true but I didn't let him suspect my thoughts as I wanted him to carry on.

'Have you spoken about it to Patrick?' I asked innocently.

'Yes, and he denies knowing anything.'

'Who pays the bills for large cheques like that?' Without waiting for his answer I added, 'I hope it's you.'

'No,' he said, tapping his pen. 'Patrick pays all the bills.'

'Yes, but not amounts like £70,000.'

'Oh, no, I only let him sign cheques up to £50,000.'

'*Fifty thousand?*' I squeaked. 'I told you before you even took over not to let *any* employee be a signatory. You had Nigel, and now it's you and your wife. That was enough. Don't you remember I warned you of this very thing. And you're supposed to be a businessman.'

I shook my head in disbelief. Colin flushed with annoyance.

'How did he manage to sign for £70,000 if £50,000 was his limit?' I asked.

'He forged my signature.'

'Oh, come on.'

He looked annoyed that I didn't go along with this rubbish. I noticed he didn't say that Patrick *must* have forged his signature, but that he actually had, as if it were a fact. A pretty strong accusation.

Finally, I said, 'I don't believe Patrick stole, embezzled – call it what you like – any money, let alone a sum like that. He could be found out too easily. But he wouldn't anyway. I always found him completely honest.'

'It couldn't have been anyone else.' Colin sounded quite definite. 'No one else has access to the cheque book. He also changed all the suppliers without my knowledge or approval shortly after we took over. I couldn't understand why. It was only recently that I discovered it was because he was getting backhanders from the new suppliers.'

Colin's revelations were beginning to make me feel sick.

'And there was the matter of a property deal,' Colin went on. 'He—'

'Don't tell me any more,' I cut in. 'I don't want to hear it.'

He rambled on in spite of my asking him not to but I closed my ears.

Until I heard,

'… so if you think we can work together to pull the business round, Denise, I would very much like to try … if you think, after all that's happened, you can work with me.'

I was stunned. Had I heard right? Work with Colin? It was the last thing I wanted to do. I despised him. I couldn't hack seeing him every day. Not even one day. Not even ten minutes. Yet it might be the only way I could get my money. At least I'd be able to see the monthly income and expenses which I'd not had sight of for some time and see if they were as bad as Colin had indicated. All this was flying around in my head while Colin was looking at me expectantly.

'I'm not sure,' I said, still not believing I'd heard right. 'This has come out of the blue. I don't know how it would work at all. How do you see it?'

'You can share my office…'

Ugh. Working side by side on Nigel's faux cherrywood desk repelled me. I tried not to show my revulsion.

'I'd probably be more useful nearer the staff,' I said, the situation so surreal I couldn't believe I was suggesting how we'd go about working together. 'I could get a proper feel as to how they're operating, and what the costings are, and all the other figures. I'd need to see regular statistics as per the contract.' I looked directly at him.

He didn't bat an eyelid. He just said: 'Of course. You must see whatever you need to. Nothing will be kept from you. Do you think you could do it?'

'I'll have to think about it … and maybe *if* we can do this, it must be set out in a proper businesslike way on a formal basis.'

'Of course.'

'By the way, what happened to the apartment block?' I asked.

'We let them go.'

'What do you mean?'

'We disinstructed ourselves.' Colin said this with a kind of pride.

My mouth dropped open. 'Why, for God's sake?'

'We found Timothy impossible to work with.'

'He's one of the nicest developers I've ever known,' I said, not bothering to hide my incredulity. 'Absolutely straight, reasonable … I don't understand.'

'You must respect my decision.' Colin's tone was also beginning to sound edgy.

'You were joint agents.' I couldn't shut up. 'Even if you left it for the other agent to sell all of them, and not do any work at all, you would have still picked up half the commission. It doesn't make sense.' I looked him in the eye, and he shifted his away.

I badly wanted to say I was sure it was Timothy who'd disinstructed *them*, not the other way round. But if we were to have any possibility of working together I had to button my mouth.

After three hours – yes, a three-hour meeting – I said I had to go. He got up to help me with my coat, and wait for it…

'As we're friends again,' he said, 'I think a kiss is in order.'

He was beginning to make me feel nauseous.

'I'll be in touch,' I said, twisting my head away once more, 'but I'll have to lay down some ground rules if it's to have any chance of working.'

'Fine,' he said. 'Send your proposal to me and we'll go through it. Then you can get started.'

'I haven't made up my mind I'll definitely do this,' I told him. 'It's a big thing you're asking.'

Claire, the ex-sales co-ordinator, recently told me the following story: 'Colin knew I'd originally worked for you.' (She'd started on the first day with me when I opened the first town office and I'd quickly promoted her from being a superb secretary to the tough position of sales co-ordinator. She'd left long before I sold, wanting a change after so many years, but decided to return as she missed estate agency.) 'On my first day,' she continued, 'I thought he'd call me into his office just to welcome me back. But there was no word from him for six weeks. Then one afternoon, about four o'clock, he called me into his office and did the welcome back bit for a few minutes. But then he proceeded to tell me about himself, what school he'd gone to, then on to Oxford University, his children by the first marriage, by the second, the businesses he'd set up and then sold, all the marvellous charity work he did … it went on and on. Frankly, I wasn't that interested and just wanted to get back to my job and all the phone calls I needed to make. The last hour I was actually standing in the doorway.

'When I finally managed to escape down the stairs I looked at my watch. It was almost seven o'clock and everyone had gone home. I'd had to listen to him talking about himself for *three hours*. The girls in the office had warned me that most things he told them were a pack of lies. They used to call him Walter Mitty.'

I knew she wasn't exaggerating. As you've read above, I'd had the three-hour meeting with him myself.

Although extremely sceptical, and against all advice from my sister who was horrified I should even entertain the idea, I decided I would give it a shot. You may ask if I was really taken in by far too many apologies, the sincere expression, the worried frown, the plea for help? If not, then why would I give this dog-fly the time of day? Because I wanted my money, that's why. And because this seemed like the only possible way (with the exception of a court case) to get it.

I would be paid a daily salary, give advice, train the staff and so on, and generally try to get the business back on course. From some of the statistics I'd managed to get my hands on recently it was clear that the company was beginning to go downhill. Maybe I could help it regain its reputation. If I was around it would be a boost for the staff and stop anyone from giving in their notice.

I drafted Colin a two-page letter of the terms as I envisioned them, but first sent it to James to cast his eye over it. I asked him to phone me to discuss it.

'It might be worth giving it a go,' James said. 'Maybe some kind of resolution will come from it. But I'd change a couple of points as you've been a bit strong.'

I thought I'd been scrupulously fair but on his advice I toned them down and emailed the amended one to Colin.

This might change my life yet again, I thought. I couldn't wait to see what his response would be. Sometimes I thought I was either crazy or stupid, and sometimes I thought I was being very mature and businesslike. Neither one took precedence.

It wasn't long before I found out through one of the managers that Colin had lied about the £70,000 missing cheque for the tax bill. Of course he had. Later Colin admitted to me that he had 'mislaid' the cheque and that it had now 'turned up'. Meanwhile, Colin had smeared Patrick's name.

I decided to ring Patrick and find out what had happened, even though I hadn't spoken to him since the meeting with the two solicitors. He didn't sound that surprised to hear from me.

'I couldn't stand working for him any longer,' he said, a somewhat bitter note in his voice.

I couldn't quell a jolt of pleasure.

I didn't bother to tell him Colin had told the staff Patrick had been put on garden leave for alleged misdemeanours. At the last minute I decided not to bring up Colin's accusations. It would only have infuriated Patrick and God knows what a can of worms I would have opened.

'Neither of them was like you to work with,' he admitted.

No. I'm sure they weren't.

He also told me how Colin had spread rumours about me – what a bad businesswoman I was, how I'd left all the offices in an unsafe state, how the staff disliked me … I decided I'd heard enough.

'And you won't get your money, Denise,' he went on. 'There *is* no money. The figures showed a loss of £20,000 this quarter. I don't know what they've done with it but they said they're definitely not going to give you any more.'

I wished him luck in his new venture and that was the last time I spoke to him. I never did find out whether Colin had got rid of him or Patrick had walked out.

Colin cancelled the meeting he'd agreed to have in my accountant's office to go through my proposal. He said he hadn't had enough time to read it (he'd only had it for a week and it was all of two pages).

Finally, he turned up at the next proposed date in James's office. The meeting lasted no more than a quarter of an hour.

Basically, Colin said he couldn't agree with most of the points I'd written. James tried to suggest further compromises but I threw him some black looks. I wasn't willing to negotiate as nothing I'd proposed was weighted against Colin in any way. I'd handed Colin a lifeline by giving him a longer pay-out period, thereby substantially lowering the quarterly amounts so that he could catch up with the payments and my apportionments and rent. In return I would give him my expertise. All I had asked for was that I be allowed to work in my own style (which had served me well in the past) and I was sure I could bring the business back to its full capacity. I could only achieve this with Colin's support. That obviously wouldn't be forthcoming.

Checklist:

1. Beware of very long meetings where you don't feel you are making any progress. You probably won't be. But make notes of key points. You may find them useful one day.

2. If your buyers are proving to be untrustworthy, rather than purely incompetent (or a mixture of both), it is doubtful that working together with them in the hope of recouping your money will be the answer.

FOURTEEN

Dave

Part of me was disappointed Colin hadn't gone along with my proposal, but it really wasn't unexpected. To be honest, I felt relieved that I wouldn't have to face him on a daily basis. In my heart I knew it couldn't possibly work but I'd been willing to give it a try. And when I thought about it, I don't believe he had any intention of involving me in the business. It was all a sop, hoping I would delay going to court.

A few days after this ridiculous waste-of-time meeting I received an email from Colin saying that there was no Consumer Credit Licence in place when they took over. And that I was breaking the law. And that this was most serious. Was there no end to this man? I renewed this licence every year without fail and left it in the appropriate file in head office. I'd already told him before completion of the sale that I was meticulous about renewing it, and that they must continue to do so. I emailed back telling him exactly where to find the file. He wrote back ignoring this, and asked where the income was from Financial Services. I replied that if he read his contract he would see that we'd agreed I would keep any income from that department. Not that it had made any difference – to date I'd had nothing. He didn't answer.

That evening I had another phone call from one of the village landlords saying their rent hadn't been paid, and a second phone call from the bookkeeper saying Colin had instructed her not to pay me the Apportionments which we had all agreed amounted to £10,000. This amount was stated in the contract and was to have been paid on completion of the sale.

The following day James phoned me.

'I've just spoken to Colin who has quotes for the premises you own. He says the whole façade is rotten and will cost £60,000 to repair, so his claim has gone to over £200,000.'

Even James, who sometimes tried to understand Colin's point of view, seemed lost for further words.

I felt such a fool to think I could have entertained the idea of working with the man. Frankly, I was sick to death of him.

Colin decided to employ someone in Patrick's place. I had long ago realised Colin had no confidence or experience to run such a big company and needed another person to manage it and do anything unpleasant on his behalf. He took on another friend, Dave Crannerley. This was to have disastrous consequences as Dave was not only a most obnoxious person with the staff and suppliers, but also with the clients whenever he came across them. Several members of staff told me about the numerous times where he argued with clients, even shouted at them, and was constantly rude to individual employees in front of the others. Apparently, his mouth knew no bounds.

Furthermore, he had no estate agency experience. Not that that necessarily matters if you have a decent grasp of business per se. I couldn't see what he was adding to the business for his eye-popping salary, while assuring everyone he was there to save the company money. What Colin saw in him I'll never understand.

The next blow to the staff came when only a quarter of them

received any commission at the end of the previous month. This would have saved Colin in the region of £20,000 as that particular month was excellent. None of the secretaries had had any, nor the part-timers. When I owned the company, apart from paying the staff a basic salary higher than any competitor would offer (one of the best ways to keep good people), their contracts *all* included commission, though obviously on a sliding scale depending on their position and hours. That way they had an incentive to reach and even exceed their targets, and could all be part of the fun every time a house exchanged contracts. Colin couldn't see how important this was for the morale of the staff. He simply told them there was no money left in the kitty. As far as he was concerned, the employer's obligations could go out of the window.

Colin lost any vestige of respect he had ever scraped together from the staff members. One by one Dave told all the staff they would have to cut down their hours. Colin always made Dave do all the dirty work. But when the staff argued with Dave, and in desperation turned to Colin, saying that they wouldn't be able to provide a full service, Dave said there wasn't enough money coming in and the overheads were too high. Colin told them he'd paid far too much for the business which wasn't worth it. This didn't tally with the stats which Sharon sporadically sent me. They appeared to show the business was still managing to stay in profit, which would, of course, be down to the hard work of the staff.

On top of that I'd had an email from Dave introducing himself and telling me he would now be the one to send me the monthly figures, and that in anything to do with the business at all, I was to go through him.

After my repeated requests Dave finally sent the stats through to me but he called the valuations and instructions the 'pipeline'. This showed his ignorance, as the 'pipeline' (as every competent estate agent will know) comprises the sales which have been agreed, though not yet exchanged or completed. Dave had made no such column for the sales agreed, or the exchanges and completions, so I had no idea how many houses had been sold or what the commission was. There was no mention of Land & New Homes or Residential Lettings, nothing from one of the major town offices, and nothing from Financial Services. All in all it was a deficient set of figures which gave me no clue as to how the business was faring or any indication of future sales. I'm sure this was his intention.

I emailed him back asking for fuller details and pointing out that valuations and instructions did not constitute a pipeline. His emailed response indicated he was not best pleased. Here is an extract:

> Colin Dixtrow is the Managing Director and Owner of DB Estates. Colin and Colin alone is positioned to decide how this business is run. Colin has appointed me to provide statistics on the business that enables him to manage and develop the business as he wishes…
>
> I've only been in the estate agency business for 4 months and already I can tell I know more about it than you who is supposed to have been in it for 25 years. Of course valuations and listings are pipeline.

Dave was either a complete idiot where business was concerned or he was using this as an excuse not to send me the full figures so I couldn't tell what money was coming in. Probably a mixture of both. Needless to say, he never sent through any more stats.

The only way I was able to find out a little as to what was happening in the company was through Richard. The very same manager who rang me up twenty years before when I was trying to keep everything secret about opening my own estate agency, to tell me that another agent was coming into my village. Then when I had had the business for a few years we happened to sit next to one another at a tennis match. He was still working for our old company and mentioned that if I ever opened up an office in his town he'd love to manage it. Eventually, I did, and he did.

If Richard had been to a staff meeting he sometimes had a bit of information about the business – or lack of it – generated by the other offices, but never anything in writing.

I now had no idea what the company was doing, or where it was heading. But it was pointless to argue with Dave.

I was stuck.

I decided I would exercise my rights and march into the head office and demand that I be shown the figures. According to the contract, so long as I gave them twenty-four hours' notice, I had the power to ask for any or all figures pertaining to the business. I discussed it with James, who said he would come with me. He would let Colin know we'd be turning up. (To my constant irritation James used to tell me he wanted to keep the lines of communication open with Colin as he needed to be a mediator between us, and would also get more information out of him than if he acted otherwise. Maybe James was right but it used to touch on a raw nerve every time I heard him sounding friendly towards Colin on the phone. More than once James and I had a slight falling-out over it – something which had never happened in all the previous twenty years of our business relationship.)

I thought about the exercise. First of all James would charge me quite a few hundred pounds to be plucked out of his office, drive to another town, and then spend an hour or two looking through the books. Secondly, Colin might say yes but when we got there not be around. Daphne would then say she couldn't show us anything as she hadn't been instructed to do so. Thirdly, Colin might show me the door, which would not only upset me but would be incredibly embarrassing in front of the staff. I didn't want to put them in an awkward position; they had enough on their plates. In the end I decided against it.

Following Colin's and my conversation about Financial Services and the so-called disappearance of the Consumer Credit Licence, I read in the local paper that DB Estates Ltd were in partnership with a law company, and that clients would be offered a full range of financial services. In addition, it said that DB Estates Ltd had formed another new exciting partnership with a firm of surveyors.

I hadn't been informed of any of these partnerships or link-ups. The contract said no partnerships were to be made without my approval, and if any went ahead (with my written approval) I would benefit from the same percentage as the regular turnover. Guess why I hadn't been told?

But if Colin didn't have the Consumer Credit Licence, which you had to renew annually, he was operating against the law. And it was only a few days since he'd insisted I hadn't provided one. Presumably the link-up with these companies had been done some time ago, and the financial services carried out through DB Estates Ltd were already in operation. I'm amazed they didn't check him as they were always hot on making sure I had the Consumer Credit Licence up to date, and in a filing cabinet where other members of the staff could produce it should I not be around.

As usual, Colin was sailing very close to the wind.

Checklist:

1. If you do not have a good relationship with your buyers, think carefully before you exercise your rights. It could lead to embarrassing situations, possibly involving the staff.

FIFTEEN

Spurious claims

As my solicitor had warned, several months went by before we were able to apply for judgment on the so-called breach of the warranties. Instead of being able to enjoy my new career as a writer I still had the worry of the business, the staff in particular. Every few weeks my solicitor would be in touch to let me know the progress but it was painfully slow.

Two years had passed from the time I'd sold. I was sitting in Mark's office on a warm July morning in 2007 when, while flicking through the papers once again, he spotted something that caused him to give a little smile.

'I've just read something which I knew about when I first went over your file but it didn't really register as the date was such a long way away. But now the time is almost up and if we wait a little longer...' He showed me a clause in the contract. If the buyers hadn't claimed any of the warranties by two-and-a-half years after the sale had been completed, they couldn't claim at any later date. The deadline was 30 November 2007.

'Do you think Colin is aware of this?' he asked.

'I've no idea.'

'Well, I think it's worth waiting a few more months. We've waited this long – a bit longer probably won't matter.'

As it turned out, we should have acted immediately. But how does one know? A solicitor can only judge and give you what they consider to be the best advice. I didn't blame him or myself.

I came home from my holiday in Greece on 4 December to find a letter waiting for me. It was from Colin, dated (you've guessed it) 30 November 2007. Here it is, word for word, with all the text in italics as created by Colin.

DELIVERED BY HAND

Dear Denise

I am conscious that the Agreement between us signed May 2005 requires formal notice of warranty claims to be given to you by the end of this month.

As you are aware DBEA Ltd has the following warranty claims which are outlined on pages 2 and 3 of this letter.

Schedule 9 of the Agreement provides that warranty claims shall be deducted from the final instalments of the price.

As you are also aware, it is my wish to deal with the warranty claims as part of a negotiated final payment to you.

Yours sincerely

....

Managing Director

Warranty claim as of 2006 £206,359

Increased cost of work in 2008 @ 10 per cent across the board 20,636

Removal from 6 locations of DB's paperwork 2,500

Storage of DB's paperwork 5 years 19,200

Measurable cost of Patrick, GM (commissions) Note 1 130,000

Consultant cost (1 year) Note 2 100,000

Buy-out of any future warranties 50,000

TOTAL £528,695

Note 1: The General Manager, Patrick, was a critical component within the purchase of the goodwill of the business. It can be proved that Patrick, over the period April 2006 through May 2007, either through premeditated fraudulent action or gross incompetence, paid the staff at DB Estates in excess of £130,000 in overpayments of their commission.

Note 2: Without access to undertake due diligence, the purchaser of the business was solely reliant on the warranties provided. Due diligence would have shown that the underlying foundation of the business was, at best, fragile. The GM had no practical systems in place, the Branch Managers had no idea regarding management (having never been given a moment's management training). It has been necessary (in fact, critical) to appoint the services of a Business Consultant to assist the Managing Director in initiating systems and processes to provide a proper foundation for this business. Had the commission overpayment situation not been rectified by the Business Consultant in July, this company would have gone bust.

Further examples of aspects of this business which, if uncovered by due diligence, would have significantly reduced the buying price:

The computer system – a significant ongoing cost to the business, not one single member of staff had been adequately trained in its use. Staff training costs have NOT been included within the warranty claim.

Lettings: The purchaser was led to believe that the value of the Lettings business was in the region of £100,000. DB was quite clearly not in a position to sell this business when it was sold as her bank account had to be maintained alongside the buyers. Even now, with a dedicated team of 4 staff, lettings are only generating £140,000, not yet fully covering its cost.

Financial Services: The FS that were supposedly in place consisted of 3 staff located at the top of the town. However, the purchaser never saw any paperwork supporting this operation and indeed never saw any revenue.

Management Structure: In a 'Sales' environment (which Estate Agency is) it would be reasonable to expect that the primary role of the General Manager would be to manage and direct the sales (i.e. Manage the Branch Managers). Rather than this, the GM's time was taken with producing meaningless graphs and charts and organising suppliers to the business in which the GM was paid commission – at best, unethical.

Staff Welfare: There were no job descriptions in place. There was no staff appraisal system in place. There was no recruitment policy in place. Personnel management was non-existent.

What a Mickey Mouse report. And trust Colin to act in practically the last hour of the two-and-a-half years since he'd owned the company – the same length of time he'd been given to put in any claim, even though he said he'd been storing my paperwork for the last *five* years. He must have been laughing his head off knowing my solicitor was just waiting for this date to come and go.

As it was, Mark said we could get round the letter being dated on the last day because I was away on holiday at the time of the so-called hand delivery (I had the airline ticket to prove it) and in any case, how could Colin prove he delivered it on the 30th? I found out later he'd got one of the girls to drop it through my letterbox but there was nothing on the actual envelope to say it was a hand delivery.

The above claims were all spurious. I'd run a successful business with good staff who'd been with me for years and were fully trained on the new computer system; I'd kept an up-to-date staff manual, and I'd seen it through a four-year recession, and had the accounts year by year to prove the figures.

The total costs Colin was claiming meant I owed *him* money. Over half a million.

Checklist:

1. It is not always wise to wait for more time to roll by before acting. Check all the possible ramifications of waiting. Delaying matters can sometimes backfire.

2. Never underestimate the intelligence, or wiliness, of your buyers.

SIXTEEN

Angry landlords

I looked at my latest bank statement. No rent had been paid in for the only office I owned. It should have been £3,000. There was no explanation so I emailed Sharon. She emailed back to say it was an oversight.

Colin's claim on the condition of my freehold office was bugging me. I kept changing my mind about what to do. He was trying to frighten me, so should I ignore him? Or should I have it inspected? In the end I decided that perhaps I'd better. There was a lot of glass in the office though I was sure the façade was not about to collapse. Still, it wouldn't hurt to have it checked. I can't believe, as I write this, that I spent even more money to prove that my premises were sound.

Of course, this was a perfect excuse for Colin not to pay my rent. Funny, if it was so dangerous, and I was contravening Health & Safety, he was apparently still happy to let everyone carry on working there.

I had a call on my home telephone number. It was one of the village landlords.

'Denise, could you speak to Colin?'

I just knew what was coming.

'I haven't had my rent for the last quarter.'

'I'm sure it's an oversight,' I said, using Sharon's words to me, needing to keep up the pretence that I had sold to perfectly normal, reasonable buyers.

'I'm not so sure,' he said, surprisingly. 'There are rumours going around that they're in financial difficulties.'

'Really?' I feigned ignorance though I wasn't sure if this was the right tactic. Should I let him know I was worried myself? I'd known this landlord for a long time and we'd become friends over the years. After a few moments debating with myself I decided not to say anything detrimental about them.

'I've heard it from several different sources,' he went on. 'No smoke without fire, and all that. Especially when I haven't been paid. Makes you wonder, doesn't it? But then, you'd be the first to know if they were in trouble, wouldn't you?'

That's where you're wrong.

'I'll have a word,' I promised.

A few days later I received another call from a second landlord saying the same thing. This one was not so friendly.

'You realise you're the guarantor?' he said. 'If they don't pay up in a fortnight I will be looking to you for my money.'

No quarterly payments, no rent coming in, and now I was being threatened to pay *their* rent arrears.

I sighed. 'I'll talk to them,' I said.

I sent an email to Colin about the rent arrears from the two landlords and reminded him I hadn't had my rent either. Dave rang me in response.

'I'm having to juggle bills at the moment,' he said, and rang off before I could think of a reply.

Mark phoned.

'I think you should prepare a full statement for the court,' he said. 'And I do mean "full". Tell the whole story from the start to the present, in detail. You might not have to read any of it out, and the judge might not read it, but it's all there if we need it. Make sure you get your facts right.'

'How long do you expect it to be?' I asked.

'At least twenty-five pages.'

'Twenty-five pages?' I squeaked.

It ended up at thirty-two pages.

It came in jolly handy when writing this book.

Checklist:

1. Keep ALL documents, emails, reports, diaries etc. to do with
   the sale of your business both before and after completion.
   You never know when these records might prove crucial for
   writing up a court statement, or indeed being vital in the
   defence of any action for libel or slander.

SEVENTEEN

Spilling the beans

I was becoming desperate. Payments were still not forthcoming and I had no contact now with Colin. Everything, Colin told me via email, had to be through Dave.

I decided to see if I could get an appointment with their bank manager. Yes, I knew this was not a normal approach but I needed the bank to know what was going on. After all, I figured I'd been one of their best customers for twenty years. Surprisingly, I was granted an interview with Mr Chakrajevan.

'As you will understand, Denise, I can only listen to you,' he said, squaring up a couple of folders on his desk. 'I can't make any comments as Colin is now my customer.' He didn't mention Nigel.

'Yes, I do realise,' I said, humbly, 'and I'm really grateful for a chance to talk to you.'

I proceeded to tell him in detail the whole sorry story. How well the business was doing, that the figures were holding up and yet I was not getting paid. Mr Chakrajevan sat so still that when he finally spoke I jumped.

'Starting up a new business is very costly.'

I closed my eyes briefly in despair. Was it me who was being completely unreasonable?

The bank manager was saying more or less the same thing

as my original solicitors, which was one of the reasons I'd changed to Mark.

'It can hardly be called a new business,' I reminded him, a decided edge to my tone. 'They've been trading for two-and-a-half years and I left them with half a million in the pipeline.'

Mr Chakrajevan didn't answer.

'Do you have regular meetings with Colin?' I asked.

There was a pause before he said he did.

'When you discuss the monthly figures, don't you point out that there are no payments made to me, even though the turn-over and profit margin are more than he and I had forecasted?'

'I can't answer that.'

'So you're not bothered at all that Colin isn't fulfilling his legal commitment to me?'

'I can't answer that.'

'Not being able to answer leads me to think you don't question him,' I said. 'But surely it's your responsibility to see that he meets his financial obligations. You knew I was supposed to have regular quarterly payments.'

He sat like a statue. I never realised how difficult it is to have a completely one-sided conversation about something impor-tant. I plunged on, desperate for some kind of response.

'I only hope you're not seeing me as some kind of vindictive female, but I want you to understand I *am* going to take this further. I wanted to warn you so that you would speak to Colin. Let him know I'm dead serious. Will you at least do that?'

He said he would be seeing Colin presently but refused to say what they would be discussing.

'I don't trust Colin,' I said. 'And I don't think I'm going to get my money. I've had to threaten to sue them each time on the few payments I have had.'

Mr Chakrajevan didn't even blink.

'If I don't receive a payment soon I'm *definitely* going to make Colin bankrupt,' I flashed. Surely *that* would make Mr Chakrajevan sit up and take notice. And do you know what he said?

'I think he's doing his best considering the business is so new. *I've got a lot of time for Colin.*'

I was astounded that Mr Chakrajevan, a senior bank manager, was well and truly hoodwinked, and obstinately refused to believe anything I'd told him.

I rose to my feet. What more was there to say?

Shortly after that meeting I was sickened to see what I secretly termed as my 'posh' village office close. This closure led to a major disinstruction. It was a row of very pretty, converted listed cottages on that particular office doorstep. I had been in touch with the developer for the last five years, working closely with him all through the planning application and advising on the way he was going to convert them into comfortable homes. We were just about to put them on the market when I sold the company. Everyone wanted a cosy beamed cottage with an open fireplace, but with the convenience of a new kitchen and bathroom. They'd be snapped up. Yet again Colin and Nigel would reap the benefits.

Almost immediately after the office closed I had a phone call from the developer saying he had disinstructed my old company.

'The main reason you were going to have the business, apart from all the work you did beforehand, was because your office was right opposite,' he said. 'Now it's gone and so are you, so I'm taking the business elsewhere.'

'I'm still involved,' I tried to argue, but it was useless.

'I'm sorry, Denise. I've heard you've sold to a couple of muppets, and I've made my decision.'

The commission was worth somewhere in the region of £50,000. Another agent sold the lot in a matter of weeks. I could have wept.

Swiftly on the heels of the closure of that office, which by the way was extremely profitable because the overheads were low and the houses were expensive, went what was my jewel in the crown: Country Homes. That was where we would get the cream of the properties. Houses over a million would bring in welcome weighty cheques.

Dave told the managers it was an unnecessary expense and that the offices were all capable of dealing with the large houses. Not so. You need that special knowledge of period homes, plus it doesn't hurt to have the right accent. (Not PC, I know, but talk to any of the big London agents and you will hardly understand them, their mouths are so full of plums.) You also need a confident air to persuade the sellers they didn't need to instruct the London boys with their shiny brochures and even shinier motors to get a good purchaser at the best price. It's all about perception. Sellers want to know their up-market houses are treated in a special way, and that means more select advertising and promoting within a dedicated department.

When I opened Country Homes we immediately attracted substantial quality properties between £1 million and £2 million. Now it was all down the drain. The new company never again took instructions for another prestigious house of a million or more. In fact, the most expensive was £750,000. All this, of course, would have an adverse effect on the company's revenue which would have a knock-on effect on me. Well, it would have done if they'd been paying me, but because they didn't, it didn't, if you see what I mean.

Land & New Homes was another one to go. Although it had

never had its own separate building, we used to have a proper boardroom where we could talk to developers and pore over house plans – essential for providing a professional environ- ment, as we were in competition with so many other agents in town who pushed hard to win these multiple and lucrative units. A new development was a real feather in the cap for any agent with its myriad marketing opportunities. But now there was no special designated office to engage with the prospective developer. I was certain they'd never be given another site.

Unfortunately, I was proved right.

As if they were on a roll they closed the newest office I'd opened right before I sold. This was the one set up especially for first-time buyers, and it was beginning to dovetail in with the other offices. The younger buyers loved it as they felt comfortable in the informal atmosphere. I thought that would be it until I saw Colin had closed my lovely Residential Lettings office. They said they were going to put one Lettings person into every branch. They tried it. Of course it didn't work because that employee would be working on her own. She would have no one to talk over problems with, come up with ideas, or cover for her when she was out of the office. Colin lost a whole load of income through that pointless exer- cise and Lettings was never as prominent again.

They were down from eight offices to four.

Three of the more mature ladies who had been with me for years and were excellent at their jobs then got a nasty shock. Dave walked into each one's office one day and told them they were redundant with immediate effect. They were told to pack up their desks and leave on the spot. How cruel. How much more short-sighted could Colin get? These women had few family responsibilities, they were punctual, rarely sick, and were generally of the old school in their conscientiousness and expertise. I valued them highly. Now they were regarded as worthless because of their age.

Word had got around that the management didn't want 'old' people and not only that, but negotiators with experience of selling property were too expensive and not necessary: they only needed to be salespeople, and it didn't matter what they had been used to selling. It could be selling cars or ice cream – it was all the same. And you wouldn't have to pay them such ridiculously high salaries and commissions.

The women who lost their jobs were in tears and phoned me but there was nothing I could do. I was so upset for them as they had given me such loyal service. One of them, I knew, was very hard up so I sent her a cheque to help cover her family's food and utilities for a few months. But all they really wanted was their jobs back.

A few weeks later I was alarmed to find out that there was another wave of redundancies. This time it was four bright, hardworking and loyal women. Three of them called me. One was crying. When I asked them what had happened they said Dave had told them they were now redundant. No warning, either verbally or in writing. When they'd tried to speak to Colin he had given them no explanation, only said that Dave was in charge of personnel. I told the girls if Dave said *they* were redundant it was illegal; it's not the employee who is redundant, it's the job. They were all lovely girls who had been with me for years.

I blamed Dave at the time, but on reflection it was down to Colin. He was the director and therefore he had the last word.

I advised the girls to take legal advice.

This time I really couldn't understand why Colin had let these women go; they were only in their forties. Their redundancies were definitely illegal because less than a month later new people filled their positions. It then dawned on me that Colin was using Dave to gradually get rid of my original people and replace them with inexperienced ones more suited to Colin's method of operation.

Two of the women told me they were definitely going to take Colin to a tribunal for unfair dismissal, but when it came to it they changed their minds. They sadly told me they couldn't afford the solicitor because if they didn't win they hadn't got that sort of cash to pay the fees their solicitor had outlined. I told them there were other solicitors around who wouldn't charge if they lost the case and they promised to look into it and keep in touch. In the end I don't think they could take the emotional pressure. And I couldn't blame them. It was such a shame as it was so obvious they would have won the case. Of course, this was just what Colin was banking on.

Checklist:

1. Don't rely on a bank manager to make judgements of character.

2. If any ex-employee says they have been illegally or unfairly made redundant, you can advise them to speak to ACAS (Advisory, Conciliation and Arbitration Service), mentioning they are employed with the new owner under TUPE. ACAS is extremely helpful – and free.

EIGHTEEN

Where's their defence?

'**E**ven closing one office constitutes a material change,' Mark said at one of our meetings. 'And they've closed four. Furthermore, they're five payments behind so far. It's time we sued again.'

I agreed.

Mark wrote to tell me he had given them seven days to pay me. If the money was not forthcoming, he would apply for a court hearing without further notice.

I persisted in asking Dave to send me the statistics. A fortnight after my latest request I had an email from him telling me that as I was issuing proceedings against the company I should now do everything through my lawyer. He confirmed he wouldn't be sending me any more statistics.

Mark phoned to say that the defendants intended to defend against all the claims we had made. No surprise there. But what annoyed me was that Colin had asked for an extension of several weeks and had been granted it by the court. I wrote in my diary:

I think I will go mad with all this waiting, which is of course exactly what Colin wants.

And then, can you believe, when the time was almost up, Colin asked for a second extension? And he got it. Even Mark

was astonished – he said you have to have a very good reason
to apply for more than one extension. That reason has to be
that Colin has a defence. Yet if he had a defence he should have
submitted it by now. The judge granted him a second extension without a defence. This was almost unheard of.

Colin then pushed his luck and, through his solicitor, asked
us for a *third*. By this time I was tearing my hair out. Apparently
my solicitor had the power to say no at this point so naturally
he did. But Colin took no notice: he simply let us know that he
was going to apply direct to the court. Why was it that Colin
always knew exactly how far he could go? Could he and Nigel
have done this sort of thing before?

Mark heard from Mr Fritch, who admitted that Colin didn't
have a defence but he still wanted to put in his counter-claim
(which was now out of time) for £140,000. The amount
changed almost weekly. It had gone down from £528,000 to
this £140,000, the latter being the original amount that Nigel
concocted when he did the survey of the offices four months
after taking over. Colin hadn't included the so-called £100,000
calculated for the village office I owned (which in their words
was 'falling to bits'), nor anything else on that ridiculous list.

The next thing I heard was that all the remaining offices
were having an expensive computer system installed. The
current one was still only three years old and, according to all
the surveys on the subject, was reputed to be top drawer. Even
more importantly the negotiators loved it and told me they
dreaded another new system. It just wasn't necessary when
theirs was working so well and did everything they needed.

Colin got a further seven days. Mark was astounded. He said
he'd never known such a thing. Colin and his solicitor said they
required the extra time as they had another 'expert' (presumably

a surveyor) who would go round all the offices and come up with a figure to cover all that needed doing on the properties. They expected it to be about £140,000, so they had to make sure their expert came up with the same figure they were suing me for. It makes you wonder about the integrity of their expert, doesn't it?

We received the report which, surprise, surprise, was calculated to be exactly £140,000 worth of outstanding works. So spending even more money, I had to ask my independent surveyor if he would look through the report and comment on every point.

That night I wrote in my diary:

Colin is making a lot of money with Financial Services. He knows perfectly well that I am supposed to have my share of FS income. I managed to get sight of one of the Managers' Minutes which clearly stated that FS is part of DB Estates. The FS man actually thanked everyone for the amount of leads which have come through – around fifty in the last six to seven weeks since he has been on board.

Cheque came in today for the rent of my village office. Stunned, I took it to the bank, wondering if it would clear.

Incredibly, it did.

Checklist:

1. Even though counter-claims can be 'out of time', be warned, the judge may still take them into consideration.

NINETEEN

Desperation

Colin's latest was that all the windows in all six offices were apparently dangerous because they were not safety glass. He presented me with another huge bill to have them all replaced. Was he trying to send me barmy? I was forced to take action yet again.

Bob, the man from the glazing company, sounded surprised. 'You're Denise Barnes, the estate agent, aren't you?'

I agreed that I was.

'We did several of your windows when you set up twenty years ago, and checked most of the others when you expanded. What's the problem?'

'I'm having difficulty with my buyers,' I explained. 'They say the premises are unsafe and it's partly due to the windows.'

'I doubt that very much but I'll have a look at them by the end of the week,' he promised.

I suddenly thought of something. 'Do you have to go inside?'

'No, not at all. But I'll put my head in the door and tell everyone who I am. We don't want to alarm them because there's some guy out there measuring the windows for no good reason.'

I thought this sounded OK. Colin and his henchman were normally huddled on the second floor in their office. With luck, they wouldn't notice anyone lurking outside.

On Friday afternoon I had a phone call from the glazing company.

'Ms Barnes, it's Bob. We've had a look at all your windows in every office. I'm pleased to say they're all within safety standards. The only exception is the listed building and you have to keep those exactly as they are. But they're not dangerous in any way.'

'That's great news,' I said, 'though not for you.' He chuckled. 'Could you send me your report so I can use it as evidence? And the bill, and I'll get the cheque off right away.'

'Just one other thing...' Bob hesitated. 'At your main branch a bearded chap came rushing down the stairs, tore open the front door and asked me what the hell I was doing. I explained but he said, "Clear off, and don't come back. And I forbid you to set foot in any of the other premises." I didn't bother to tell him I hadn't been inside and it wasn't against the law to inspect a commercial window from the outside. Luckily, he didn't realise I'd already done all the offices and that one was the last.'

So Colin had accused me of having unsafe glazing in the offices yet wasn't prepared to let me have my own expert check it.

I rang my solicitor to tell him the outcome.

'More bloody money and time wasted,' was Mark's comment. 'Let me have a copy of the report when you have it, and I'll forward it on to Fritch.'

Just as Bob said, all was in order. The report was quite detailed and I wouldn't be allowed to change the listed building's windows even if I'd wanted to.

I heard later that the girls in that office, and indeed in all the other offices, got a right telling off from Colin for having the audacity to let some stranger inspect the windows without informing him. That in future anything connected to Denise Barnes had to be approved by him.

The bill, when it came from Bob, was another couple of hundred pounds. I reckoned I'd got off lightly.

Daphne, the bookkeeper, gave in her notice. She told me she couldn't stand working for them any more.

Colin's next lie was really sick. At the Managers' Meeting Colin said I'd sold him and Nigel a business that wasn't worth anywhere near what I'd told them it was. He'd said that kind of thing before but this time he said that I'd deliberately hood-winked them. Didn't he realise how foolish it made him look in front of everyone, that he hadn't checked the figures with an accountant before buying a substantial company? But his next announcement took them all by surprise. He said that because of my deception he would be forced to reduce the negotiators' commission, and cut out the others, once again.

I can't believe there wasn't a massive walk-out. It was incred-ible what they put up with to keep their jobs. But his ongoing plan to turn the staff against me failed; they'd sussed him out long ago.

Colin was still advertising Financial Services in the offices and in some periodicals, even though there was no longer a financial services arm to the company. This is strictly against FS regulations. Also, he displayed the National Association of Estate Agents (NAEA) logo in all the office windows long after membership had expired. Although it is not a legal require-ment for the owner/director of an estate agency to belong to the NAEA, it is highly recommended, as the public then have some protection if there is any negligence from one of the staff. Colin himself was not a member, nor did he continue to

renew the senior negotiators who had always been members.
(I and several of my negotiators had been members since I first
set up as I felt it added further credence to the agency.) These
NAEA certificates, so far as the public were concerned, were
dishonest, as they pretended Colin was a member and had staff
with all the right qualifications in place.

A man from Vebra, the company who'd sold me the state-of-
the-art estate agency package for our new computer system,
called me at home. (I'm not sure how he'd got my personal
telephone number.) I'd changed over to Vebra because the
girls were concerned that the first computer system we'd had
installed was now antiquated.

You'll never guess. Or perhaps you will.

'Your buyers haven't paid the quarterly rental since they
took over,' the Vebra man told me.

Although extremely polite he said the agreement had been
set up as a Personal Guaranteed Lease Loan to me, and so I
would now have to pay it. Colin did reimburse me on two
occasions, very late, and totally ignoring the interest that had
mounted up. I paid the several remaining payments because I
didn't want to lose my credit rating.

Mark rang.

'I've had a letter from Fritch. He says his client is willing to
settle out of court.'

Oh, yes.

'What do you think I should do?' I asked him.

'I'd like to know how he's going to come up with any money
when he says you've drained him.'

'We know that's not true.'

'Maybe we should ask him what amount he's thinking of. You never know. He might surprise us.'

Just like he has done in the past.

'OK, go ahead and ask, but I shan't hold my breath.'

We never got an answer.

Richard said that at the last Managers' Meeting Colin had reiterated they had paid me in full, and well over the top of its real value. He had also reminded them they'd bought me a brand new Mini convertible. He asked the managers to let their teams know so they could squash any rumours to the contrary.

Checklist:

1. Don't throw more good money after bad. If you are having an unhappy experience with your buyers, keep alert to their every accusation. Don't be too quick to respond. They could easily be setting traps to purposely cost you more money.

TWENTY

Decline and fall

My book launch for *From Bad to Wurst,* about my time as a vegetarian cook in a sanatorium in Bavaria, was due in two days' time. Colin told his staff if anyone attended he would take a very 'dim view'.

I had invited quite a few staff who I thought might be interested but only Richard and half a dozen others turned up. The other thirty-five or so (their numbers were rapidly diminishing) were worried about being taken a dim view of, I suppose.

Two weeks later I was in Waterstones doing my first book signing when Bill Wright, a car salesman who I'd bought my Mini from, came through the doors. After kindly buying one of my books, and while he was waiting for me to sign it, he remarked: 'You might not know this but I sold Colin and Nigel their new Jaguars when they bought your business.'

'No, I didn't know. But I remember being surprised they were spending so much money before the ink had even dried on the contract. So do you still deal with them?'

'Yes. They're on a payment schedule. But listen to this … Colin rang me yesterday saying that DB Estates is heading for liquidation.'

My pen stopped in mid-air.

Even if it were true, why would Colin warn one of his suppliers in advance? And why would he tell *anyone* before telling the staff? I was sure the staff had no idea because someone would have told me. It didn't make sense. I could have cried hearing something so awful about my former estate agency from a customer in a bookshop, especially today which was supposed to be a really exciting and happy day for me.

'He told me not to worry,' Bill went on, 'but of course I am. He said he'd call me in the next two weeks to let me know what was happening.'

'He won't phone you,' I said, handing him the book, and told him a little about what had gone on since I'd sold. His jaw dropped.

'What a horrible experience,' he said. 'Can't you sue them?'

Later that afternoon I rang the bank to speak to Mr Chakrajevan to warn him of the impending liquidation. He wasn't there. I asked if I could leave a message as it was urgent I speak to him. Someone assured me they would pass the message on. Silence. I rang again the next day and still was not able to speak to him.

I phoned Richard and asked if he'd heard anything. He'd told me on more than one occasion that Colin's ineptitude, and the so-called business adviser, Dave, who was supposed to be saving the company money, resulted in the fact they were actually haemorrhaging it away. Both men were too full of their own importance, he said, to take proper professional advice.

He made the point that money was obviously tight as he knew several bills hadn't been paid such as the stationery, local newspaper advertising, the new computer system and the staff's parking spaces.

'We're even having to photocopy our headed notepaper,' Richard finished. 'It looks so unprofessional.'

That last cut-back horrified me more than their other debts. In the four-year recession I went through I would never have dreamed of doing something so tacky. Everyone's morale must be at an all-time low. How much further did they intend to sink before the inevitable crash?

I decided to see James to let him know what Bill Wright had told me. Shaking his head he grabbed the phone, and got straight through to Colin.

'I've heard a rumour that the company is on the verge of going into liquidation,' James opened the conversation.

'Not true,' said Colin. 'Who told you that?'

'I'm not going to drop anyone in it,' James said, 'but apparently the quote was from your own lips.'

'Well, we've just taken on more staff – a new lettings person started only yesterday – and although the market's difficult, we're holding up.'

'Perhaps you'd be good enough to send me the balance sheet then,' James said, and after he'd put the receiver down he went through the conversation.

'You've been asking for the balance sheet for weeks now,' I said, jotting down a few notes about the call. 'It'll be interesting to see it.'

'I wouldn't hold your breath,' James said.

The hours and days crawled by while I waited for their next move. It came one evening about a fortnight after Bill had warned me they were going bust. My phone rang. It was Richard.

'Denise, we've just been given the news that the company's going into liquidation. As from now. '

'Rotten bloody incompetent bastards,' I choked out the words, almost dropping the phone, my hands were shaking so much. 'They've ruined my lovely business. And buggered the lives of all the staff.'

You'll say I saw it coming ... indeed, was *told* it was coming, but none of the warnings had prepared me. My stomach churned and I felt I was going to throw up. I could hardly take it in that it was really happening.

'Were you called into a meeting? Or did they come round to each office?' I asked him.

'The managers were called to head office late this afternoon. Dave and Colin were there and Dave told us we were redundant and that everyone would be officially made redundant tomorrow. They swore us to secrecy not to tell our teams when we went back to the office.'

'How ridiculous.' For once I didn't have to hide the contempt I was feeling. I knew Richard felt exactly the same.

'As if we could go back and pretend everything was normal, then sock it to them the next morning,' he went on. 'We all told our teams straight away. And the vendors, of course. We'll have to phone or write to them all, and deliver their keys. Colin and Dave never think of these things. I'm staying on at the office to do this.'

Naturally he sounded worried. He had a family with two daughters at university.

'What about your salary?'

'We've been promised this month that we've worked,' he said. 'Legally, I think they'll have to give it to us.'

Colin wouldn't if he could possibly get away with it. But I didn't say anything.

'I'll let you know what happens tomorrow.' He rang off.

I spent a horrible night going over and over everything. Was I to blame at all? But what could I have done? They simply hadn't wanted me around to give them any help or advice. They were also aware that I would have constantly reminded them they hadn't paid me. From their point of view I was best kept right out of the way.

I worked it out that it was three years almost to the day when I'd sold.

Richard rang me the next morning. He sounded exhausted.

'I stayed in the office late last night to contact all my vendors … and the buyers as well. Then I delivered all the keys. Everyone's in shock. One day they have a job, next thing they've got nothing. It's a nightmare. I think you'll be receiving some phone calls from some of them.'

'What are you going to do?' I asked him.

'I've got a couple of ideas,' he said. 'Do you fancy having a chat over a coffee?'

Richard had chosen a restaurant along the road from his old office and we sat for an hour or two with our coffees. He told me how he'd seen this coming for some time and had been seriously thinking about starting his own agency. He put down his cup, looked me in the eye, and said:

'Do you fancy coming in with me?'

'What, to start up again?'

Richard nodded.

I really wasn't prepared for this. But I knew the answer.

'Definitely not,' I said. 'The last thing I want to do is go back into estate agency. All that stress. The weekly migraines. No thank you.'

He looked a little disappointed, then almost seemed to brighten.

'What about all the leases you've been left with?'

'Well, yes, they're a big problem,' I admitted. 'The head office is nearly forty grand a year and runs another twelve years. And there are four others with years still left to go. And there's my own office. I'll have to re-let that as well.' I suddenly felt I needed something stronger than a coffee when I thought of such a dismal future ahead of me.

'It's not going to be easy in this market to get rid of them all,' Richard commented.

I had to agree.

'If you can't find new tenants it'll be a huge financial burden for you, won't it?' he persisted.

I could see where he was going. 'About a hundred grand a year.'

Richard sucked in a builder-type breath. 'Is that including the rates?'

Oh, my God, I hadn't thought of the bloody rates.

I shook my head.

'You can add another thirty grand at least to the hundred,' Richard said.

'It's never-ending.' My shoulders slumped as I breathed out a deep sigh. 'They're in arrears with half the rents and I've already got the landlords breathing down my neck. *And* they haven't paid *me* any rent for the last two quarters. At this rate it won't be long before I'm bankrupt myself.'

'So will you at least think about it?'

'Richard, if I was your age (he's twelve years younger) I would say "yes" immediately and be up for the challenge. But I'm serious about my writing, and not just as a hobby.'

We talked some more and believe it or not I began to get caught up with some of his enthusiasm and ideas. He said *if* we did it we would only keep two offices – the ones we'd always been in so we had the full local knowledge – his in his old town, mine in the village where I'd first started. The strain wouldn't be so bad as there'd be two of us instead of everything on my head. I could go part-time after a couple of years if I wanted ... then end up more or less as a consultant.

On the third caffeine shot, without thinking it through carefully, I said:

'I'll do it, but only two to three years. Probably only two. Then I'll want you to buy out my share, but at least it might give me the chance to earn some of the money I didn't get from that pair of sharks. And maybe I can start getting rid of the leases.'

To my astonishment he immediately agreed.

It wasn't what I'd wanted at all, but nor did I want to go bust myself. Let alone being financially wiped out, my ego couldn't have stood it. But there was something more than just trying to recoup some of my money I'd lost – it might be a way to prove to myself that I could run a successful business again from the very ashes Colin and Nigel had left us with. Phoenix rising, and all that.

Checklist:

1. When you need to make a business decision that will have a
   significant effect on your personal life, think about it carefully. Make a list of the pros and cons. You need to take it
   seriously and not decide over a cup of coffee. Always sleep
   on a major decision. Talk it over with family and/or someone you trust. It's rarely a matter of life or death if you wait
   a few days before giving an answer.

TWENTY-ONE

A surprising offer

My sister, Anna, was flabbergasted when I told her I was going to set up again, even with Richard as a partner, whom she knew to be decent and hardworking.

'Your migraines will start again (she was right) and you'll be tied to it. You won't have time to do any writing which is one of the main reasons why you sold. It's the worst thing you could have told me. Please think about it very carefully.'

The only other person who advised me not to start it up again was a lovely woman, also a writer. We'd got to know one another through my University Women's Club in Mayfair. She was sure I'd be able to get rid of the leases without too much of a problem. But she was a New Yorker. The state of the housing market had hit hard this time in the south-east. I could see more and more empty commercial premises in the high streets and knew it wouldn't be easy.

The law should be changed. At the moment it doesn't matter how many times a commercial lease changes hands, the original lessee is financially responsible. Some people have lost all their savings and homes because of a solicitor suddenly popping up and demanding on behalf of their client (the ingoing tenant) that the original owners pay up for a lease which they'd thought they'd got rid of twenty or thirty years before. This happened to a couple I knew of who were actually living their dream in Spain. After a blissful fifteen years they had to return to England, broken-hearted and penniless.

Other friends and family could understand my decision and encouraged me to go ahead, knowing I was at such financial risk with the blessed leases. But I knew Anna was thinking of my health and my freedom. She knows me better than anyone. In the end she said: 'Whatever you decide, I'll support you, but I still hope you'll change your mind.'

Two days later I had a call from James. I'd been keeping him posted with developments. Rightly or wrongly, depending upon which way you looked at it, he'd been a link between Colin and me, setting himself an impossible task. But even he surprised me by his next question.

'I don't want you to be annoyed (of course I knew by his tone I was going to be), but Colin and Dave want to meet you and Richard to talk about the demise of the company. Will you do that?'

What?

I was speechless. When I didn't answer he said, 'I think you should see them.'

I couldn't believe James was asking me to agree to such a request.

'Why? What good can it possibly do?'

'I'm not sure at this juncture, but it will be interesting to hear what they've got to say,' he said. 'I've spoken to Richard and he's willing to listen. I suggest we hold it in my office as I think I should be there as mediator. But if we do this, don't make any sarcastic remarks.' He sounded very firm. 'Just listen.'

'When do they want to meet?'

Was this really me speaking?

'Tomorrow, at five o'clock.'

A familiar feeling of nausea swept through me.

‡

Richard and I turned up at my accountant's early, determined to get there before Colin and Dave. I felt quite peculiar as I sat there in James's office, my heart hammering away with only the *idea* of seeing them.

'I'll do most of the talking,' James said. 'Just hear them out. But don't get angry or start arguing, Denise. I know what you're like.'

'I'll be the meek little woman in the background,' I assured him. 'But I still don't understand what this is all about. What can Colin and Dave possibly have to say to me? And Richard?'

I heard their footsteps coming up the stairs. And when they made their entrance I thought I would throw up. Colin bounded in, smartly dressed in suit and tie as usual, and beaming at us as though we were all best friends. Dave was his normal unattractive self, several buttons deliberately open at the neck of his shirt revealing a white flabby chest I'd have preferred not to look at. A few buttons strained over his stomach where more flesh squeezed out.

I could hardly bear to look at their faces.

James shook hands and indicated for them to take a seat. Colin put his hand out to me but I pretended not to see it. Then Dave tried.

I'd rather shake hands with a sewer rat, I almost said, and was pleased to see that Richard made no attempt at any convivialities either.

As usual, Dave did practically all the talking while Colin just glanced at the three of us every so often, presumably trying to read our expressions. I sat there stony-faced, and Richard looked suitably bland.

'You know of course that the company has gone into liquidation,' Dave began.

'No surprise there,' I couldn't resist.

Dave threw me a look with those cold fish eyes, then said, 'Colin has a proposal to make.'

'Could Colin maybe speak for himself?' I couldn't keep the sarcasm out of my tone. James threw me a warning look which I ignored.

Colin sat snapping the end of his pen. Finally, he said, 'It's best if Dave explains. He's the business adviser.'

I don't know how I stopped myself from throwing my head back and roaring with laughter. Even James looked sceptical.

'Colin proposes to sell you the business,' Dave said, watching me without blinking.

I nearly fell off my chair.

'I hardly think you have anything to sell,' I managed to splutter, focusing on Colin.

Colin slid a sideways glance at Dave.

'Please have the courtesy to listen,' Dave said, leaning forward. The small movement sent the buttons over his stomach into a frenzy.

Courtesy? This was ripe, coming from him. But I nodded for him to continue.

'We've worked out the figures – what there is in the pipeline. The equipment, computers etc. The goodwill.'

Was I really hearing this? Were they complete imbeciles as to imagine I might think there was a shred of goodwill after they'd successfully destroyed everything I'd built up?

'Your idea of a pipeline is slightly different from mine,' I said, glaring at Dave. 'A few dozen valuations won't produce any income.'

He threw me a look of contempt but didn't argue.

'What sort of a sum are you thinking of?' James enquired, leaning casually back in his chair, figures clearly at the fore-front of his accountant's mind.

'Seventy thousand pounds.' Dave looked at us as though he'd pulled a hat-trick.

Are they completely mad?

Out of the corner of my eye I saw Richard's jaw drop.

'Sorry to disappoint,' James interjected, 'but a) I don't think it's worth it – there's little, if any, goodwill for a start, and b) legally, I don't think you have the right to sell it.'

But Dave wasn't about to be stymied by that.

'Oh, the transaction would all take place here,' he said. 'The money would be passed under the table, so to speak.'

Yes, he actually used those words: 'under the table'.

My accountant raised both eyebrows and said something non-committal.

Just to see exactly where this was leading I said, 'You must be joking. It's not worth a fraction of £70,000.'

Dave threw a glance at Colin, who nodded.

'What about £10,000?' Dave said, showing his teeth in a fearsome smile, as though that should clinch the deal.

I was about to say, 'Go to hell,' but James simply got up, told them he was sure Colin no longer had a business to sell, and showed them the door.

Richard had said very little during the meeting and I had been much more reticent than usual after my promise to James. After they'd disappeared the three of us were silent for a few seconds and then I began to laugh. The very effrontery of it tickled me and it set us all off.

'I'm surprised they tried that one, I must admit,' said my
accountant, switching off his computer for the night. 'Talk
about breaking the law. They'd have been put in choky before
the cheque hit the counter. I shall inform the bank, though.
They might be interested. And Mark, too.'

'Just as well Richard and I didn't accept their first offer,' I
said, still laughing as I retrieved my jacket. 'We would have
paid sixty grand more than we needed to.'

James smiled. The irony wasn't lost on him.

James spoke to Mark about the offer 'under the table'.

'What did he say?' I asked him.

'He said for me to tell Colin and Dave to "eff off".'

'I couldn't have put it better myself,' I grinned.

Checklist:

1. Never, EVER do any financial deal that is 'under the table'. No matter how viable it sounds, how lucrative it seems, how small (or big) it is, *it's illegal*. If you get into a situation of this kind, talk to your solicitor without delay.

TWENTY-TWO

Dealing with the media

The news broke on Meridian TV. Dave had his five minutes of fame when he appeared on the screen. He said DB Estate's demise was all down to the poor housing market. It was a brilliant excuse but incorrect as the market had only just started to rock. But what more did I expect? That he was going to say it was through greed, incompetence, indifference and inexperience that they went under? That he was sorry to have to make forty people redundant overnight?

The item on the front page of *The Courier* the following day was the startling announcement that my old company, which the journalist described as one of the leading agents in town, had gone into liquidation. It went on to reiterate Dave's statement – that it was unfortunately due to the downturn of the housing market.

I was determined to set the record straight and ring someone at the newspaper who had printed such a 'sympathetic' story. I didn't need to worry. A journalist phoned me before I even had time to look up the number.

'I believe you were the original owner of DB Estates,' he began.

'It certainly wasn't called by such a ridiculous name then,' I said. 'They altered it without my permission.'

'I wondered whether you had a different take on the story.'

When I briefly told him my side he sounded delighted, and after ten minutes of questioning said the article would be printed in the next issue.

'May I see a proof before it goes to print?' I asked. 'There are some sensitive issues involved and I'd hate for any more facts to get twisted.'

He promised faithfully he'd email me a copy and wait for my approval before it went to print and I'm pleased to tell you he kept his word.

In fact my phone didn't stop ringing for two solid days. Other newspapers wanted the story. I did give a couple of interviews but more important to me was to answer the calls from various ex-employees.

'Are you going to buy back the business?' was the main question.

I didn't want to give them any false hopes just in case Richard and I didn't or weren't able to put our plan into action.

'If I do, you can be sure I'll be in touch,' was all I felt I could say.

The landlords rang, also surprised, but not so much that they didn't remind me I was now responsible for paying the rent and rates. Oh, God, I kept forgetting the rates. That would shove the figure up even higher. Three of them confirmed that Colin was in arrears and they would send me an invoice so I could pay them what was owing, and then we'd be all nicely up to date. It sounded so innocuous until I heard the combined sum they were talking about – a mere £70,000. Then there was my own office to calculate – a loss of two quarters' rent. And as I had told Richard, the leases amounted to £100,000 a year plus rates, bringing it up to about £130,000, making a grand total of £200,000 for the first year. I needed to get rid of them fast.

One ex-manager phoned me. She was nearly beside herself. She said she'd had her own house on the market with DB

Estates and she'd just seen it listed on a new estate agency website set up under Colin's name. He hadn't had the courtesy to ask her permission but had just gone ahead and shifted the file over. I looked up the name she'd told me and there were all the houses which had previously been listed with DB Estates before they'd gone down. Colin had transferred the lot to their new company, presumably without asking the other sellers for their permission either. Unbelievable. And seeing as he had only just placed DB Estates into liquidation, I would have thought it was illegal. This was something I needed to investigate.

A few days later Richard showed me a letter he'd received from Colin. The same letter was sent to all the ex-managers telling them about their new web-based company. Would you like to be part of our new success? it said. If so, you'll be given a laptop, £750 to spend on marketing and advertising (I doubt Colin was aware that you'd only get one half-page, if you were lucky, in the local paper for that), and you'll be offered a large percentage of the commission.

Colin didn't say exactly how much the percentage would be. In the meantime, presumably while Colin was waiting for takers, Dave announced he would be doing the valuations.

Really?

'So our new venture is out of the window then?' I said to Richard. 'You'll be straight on the phone to them and ordering your new laptop.'

'Their arrogance never ceases to amaze, does it?' he replied.

I wondered if they were surprised that not one manager even bothered to answer their letter.

The more I thought about the new site they'd set up the more furious I became. The first our ex-vendors were likely to hear about what had happened to their property would be when Colin got in touch to introduce himself, if he ever did. These unsuspecting sellers would have no idea what they were letting themselves in for. I comforted myself that Colin knew as much about estate agency as would fill a Post-it note, so it was doubtful he would even get the opportunity to arrange a viewing.

However, I decided the bank might like to hear about this new site. I phoned one of the managers (not Mr Chakrajevan) and a week later he called.

'You'll be pleased to know we've closed the site down,' he said.

'Thank goodness,' I said. At least Colin hadn't got away with that scam. 'Are you going after Colin and Nigel now for your money?'

'Oh, yes. We're going to pursue them.'

It was a small triumph and the one time my bank had taken any notice of me. But it was only a matter of months when the site re-opened under the same name as Dave's newborn son. Liz, the manager of our village office, came across it almost by accident. We looked at each other in amazement when we read the blurb about the new company, which ran along these lines: *Estate agents are notorious for being untrustworthy, so come to us, the agents you can trust, with a wealth of experience.*

Their only experience was walking the cheques up the hill to the bank.

Hearing us laughing, the other girls ambled over to Liz's computer to peer over her shoulder at the site. This time we saw only four houses advertised – three for sale and one under offer. We worked out by the addresses that the one under offer was Colin's, and the other three for sale belonged to Nigel, Colin's sister-in-law Sharon, and Dave. Liz clicked the mouse and the internal photographs of Colin's residence popped up.

One was his bedroom, which presumably he shared with his wife. The double bed was dressed in a cheap crumpled counterpane and on the top, artistically arranged, were three wire coat-hangers.

'The coat-hangers are obviously included in the sale.' Liz grabbed a tissue and wiped the tears running down her face. 'Part of the fixtures and fittings.'

Three years later there were no additions (of houses, not coat-hangers) and Colin's property still sported the 'under offer' sign.

Checklist:

1. If you give an interview, whether over the phone or in person, always ask to see a proof. Even though most journalists have integrity, it's surprising how the media can manipulate things, and you need to be sure they are keeping to the facts.

2. Be tenacious when you know you are in the right and report any genuine wrong-doings to the right professionals.

TWENTY-THREE

The creditors' meeting

If I hadn't been so involved I would have quite enjoyed the creditors' meeting. I'd never been to one before and am always game for a new experience. It was just a shame I was one of the main creditors, as Mark had warned me I'd get no financial settlement. The bank would be reaching out their hands first before anyone.

'I'm going to be there too,' Mark assured me on one of our phone calls.

'Do you think it's really necessary?' I said, mentally clocking up his travelling time, not to mention his hourly rate.

'Yes, I do,' his voice was firm. 'Even if it's just for moral support. But you can bet your life I'll be speaking at some point.'

Oh, well, I'd lost a small fortune already. What were a few extra hundred pounds?

On the day I was glad Mark was there. He looked very smart as he swung through the revolving doors of the hotel carrying his well-used briefcase. He was nice and early so there was plenty of time for him to talk me through the procedure.

'How many are likely to turn up?' I asked him.

'Probably no more than around fifteen. People always say they're coming but often don't bother.'

In the end there were over sixty of us. They had to turn us out of the allotted room and find a larger one. I looked around with curiosity. There were at least twenty members of staff, several landlords, suppliers, and loads of people I didn't recognise. The whole room buzzed with noise but everyone looked serious. Strangely, no one from the bank was present.

One of the organisers told me that if I was a creditor I had to sign in. She pointed to a kind of music stand near the entrance where there was a sheet pinned to it and a list of all the creditors. By the side of everyone's name was the amount owing to them in price order, so to speak. The bank topped the list with me immediately underneath, as we were owed identical amounts – £350,000. I was actually annoyed with this policy because I didn't think it right for my ex-staff and other people who knew me to know precisely my business. Personally, I think some things should remain private, but it seems everything nowadays is out on public display. (And this book goes to prove it!)

On the rostrum sat Colin and Dave and an unknown oleaginous man. No sign of Nigel. They carefully didn't look my way but instead gazed over the tops of everyone's heads as the room filled. I pointed out a table to Mark which was the nearest to the rostrum so that Colin and Dave couldn't *not* see me. Mark smirked. I could tell he was going to enjoy this.

The oleaginous man kicked off the meeting.

'Good morning, ladies and gentleman. My name is Ronald Cartwood, and I'm the liquidator who Mr Dixtrow – on my right,' he gestured, 'has appointed to represent you. I just need your consent for me to proceed.'

There was no way I wanted Colin's man to be appointed. I was about to speak up but Mark nudged me.

'Could we have a show of hands?' Mr Cartwood peered

over his spectacles, his thin lips curling up in what I supposed we were to take for a reassuring smile.

I tried to look out of the corner of my eye to see if there was any movement. Not a sign. I then quickly glanced round so I could see the whole room. Not one hand was visible. You wouldn't have heard a paperclip drop. It was almost embarrassing but Mr Cartwood didn't appear to be fazed.

'It seems you haven't quite made up your minds, so I'll carry on with the meeting and you can decide at the end.'

I thought there would be some objections but still no one said a word. Mr Cartwood shuffled his papers, cleared his throat, and began to read.

'DB Estates, formerly owned by the founder of the company, Denise Barnes, before she sold out three years ago to Colin Dixtrow and his business partner, Nigel Zennerming, has officially gone into liquidation. Ms Barnes has commenced a legal action against the company and its two directors to retrieve sums she maintains are due under the original sale contract.'

Mr Cartwood went on to fill in the financial history of the three years since I made the fateful sale to Colin and Nigel. Most of it was highly contestable, but we all sat there with glazed expressions, not believing any of it. And what was their incompetence with handling the finances to do with us anyway? We just wanted our money.

'As I mentioned, you can appoint either myself or...' he pointed to a gentleman who was sitting at the foot of the rostrum on the far side of the room, 'Andrew Gastone, who is another liquidator that the bank has sent along.'

Anyone other than Mr Cartwood.

'I now invite you to ask any questions.' He sat down, mopping his forehead. Maybe he was a little more nervous than I gave him credit for.

One of the ex-managers jumped to her feet. '*I* have several questions,' she began. 'Why did you let us all work for a whole month knowing ... *knowing* ... you were in deep trouble and couldn't possibly pay any more bills, let alone another month of salaries? You walked out with no thought whatsoever of all of us who had worked hard and loyally for you for three years, making you money which you drained from the business. You never let anyone know, including the sellers and landlords. Why didn't you warn the managers so we could have written to everyone? I went back to the office the day after you closed with my colleague and we hand-wrote notes and hand-delivered keys, using our own cars with our own petrol. I believe all the other managers did the same. You have no morals or conscience.' She sat down to wild applause.

Colin and Dave didn't even look at one another. Their faces showed no emotion whatsoever.

The next person to stand up was one of the landlords. He introduced himself, then challenged them: 'Can the two *gentlemen* tell me where my keys are and where my rent money is, and why I wasn't notified that you chose to walk out of the door leaving landlords and tenants in such a position?'

'I haven't had my key back either,' another landlord at the back shouted.

Other landlords chipped in and demanded their keys too.

Dave opened his mouth for the first time. 'Four days after we closed, Mr Dixtrow and I were sitting in the car in the car park having just bought a hundred Jiffy bags in which to return the keys. We had a phone call from the bank forbidding us any further access to the offices. So our hands were tied.'

If only that last remark were really true.

This brought a furore from the other landlords who one by

one spoke up about the appalling way this closure had been handled. They all wanted to know where their keys were and what had happened to their rent money. Dave told everyone the rent money was safe with the bank.

Then one of the landlords asked, 'Can you explain why you didn't pay the bill to renew the Tenants' Deposit Scheme which is there to protect landlords in case something like this happens?'

'I don't know anything about a Tenants' Deposit Scheme.' Dave's tone was belligerent. 'I've never even heard of it so I wouldn't know there was a renewal outstanding.'

All the landlords, realising the implication of this denial of all knowledge of the government-backed certificate, began talking at once. The landlord who'd asked the question was incredulous. 'You mean to say you've never heard of this certificate which *by law...*' he raised his voice, 'you *have* to have. If you're not in the scheme then where are you holding the tenants' deposits? Not in DB Estates, I hope.' Dave rolled his eyes. The landlord continued. 'And you didn't know the bill hadn't been paid? And you say you're a financial consultant? I run a business and I know to the day which bills are paid and which are outstanding.'

'I'm not a financial consultant,' answered Dave.

'Excuse me, what *are* you?'

'A business consultant.'

'It's the same thing. You're a disgrace to the profession and should be run out of town.'

By the way Dave's mouth twisted, I could tell he was itching to combat the remark. I had the feeling that if he and the landlord had engaged in such a conversation in a dark alley, the landlord might not have come away in one piece.

Another landlord said, 'Without this certificate it doesn't

matter in the least that the money is in the bank. It's the access we need. Without the certificate it's us landlords who'll have the full responsibility for trying to recover our money and possibly failing.'

Dave simply repeated that the money was safe with the bank. The landlords shook their heads in disbelief.

One man who was standing at the back called out, 'Why did you employ three new people at the beginning of May, one of them being my stepson who turned down a good job to come and work for your company, when you knew what was happening in the business?'

'We were still trying to save the business right up until the last minute,' Dave explained.

The same ex-manager, nostrils flaring, stood up again. 'You opened a new internet-based estate agency which you set up called 21st Century Property People. You have an office, phones, email address, website, and you advertised all the houses we had for sale *including my own* which neither I, nor to my knowledge any other seller, gave you permission to take. The sellers' contracts were with DB Estates, not with 21st Century, and *you*, Colin, transferred my house and all the other houses into your new company which is in *your* name only. You stole the business and used the money which should have been paid to your creditors *and* our salaries to fund it.'

'All we were doing,' Dave tried to soothe, 'was trying out the system by using a few examples to see if it worked.'

'I wouldn't call more than a hundred houses *a few examples*,' she said, her voice rising to a pitch. 'You were advertising all our properties on your new site with no seller's permission. That's against the law.' Her mouth tight with rage, she sat down again.

I sprang to my feet. 'There seems to be a discrepancy in

one of the dates,' I began. 'Mr Crannerley told us he and Mr Dixtrow had tried to save the company right up until the last minute. In fact they opened their new internet company at the beginning of May, almost a month before they closed DB Estates, having everything already in place, which I know only too well takes some planning. Luckily for any unsuspecting seller I reported this to the bank. They immediately had the site closed down.' I sat down to a round of applause.

Dave swung round to me. 'You're full of shit!' he fumed.

A collective gasp of horror filled the room. Mark shot up.

'You will refrain from that kind of language or leave the room,' he cautioned.

More applause.

Mark then asked, 'You say that after four days you were not allowed into any of the premises so you couldn't let anyone know. Could you tell us what has happened to the computer and main server which was removed from one of the branches shortly after closure?'

'I know nothing about it,' Dave said curtly.

'Everything will have to be put back,' Mark warned.

One creditor asked, 'Did Mr Dixtrow have full knowledge and approval of what his *business consultant* was doing, as up to now Mr Dixtrow, the *ex-director of the business*, hasn't spoken one word.'

'Absolutely,' said Colin, twirling his pen and looking up, though not catching anyone's eye. 'He had my full support in every decision.'

There was a collective rolling of eyes.

A young girl stood up. 'I worked for DB Estates,' she said fiercely. 'Like everyone else, I was given no notice or pay for the last month's work I did. I'm in rented accommodation. I've had little food since this happened. I can't pay my rent. I can't leave the house as I can't pay for petrol. What are you going to do about it? That's what I want to know. What are you going to do for me?' Her dark hair fell over her eyes as she dissolved into tears in a room which had suddenly gone quiet.

There was still no reaction from Colin or Dave.

Then another ex-employee spoke up. 'You haven't even given any of us our P45s so we can't claim our entitlement. When will we be given them?'

'Why haven't we been paid for the last month's work?' said another. 'Not only did you promise we would get it, but legally you *have* to pay.'

'What amazes me is that neither of you has apologised,' another girl spoke up. 'And neither of you has shown the slightest remorse for what you've done to all of us in this room.'

I was proud of the staff. They weren't frightened to speak out.

Still not a flicker of an eyelash from Colin or Dave.

More angry and challenging questions were fired at the two of them. At least an hour had gone by until finally Mr Cartwood said it was time to wrap it up and get on with the formal part of the meeting. Andrew Gastone was unanimously appointed by the creditors as the liquidator. Thank goodness. He explained that there was some interest in the purchase of the Residential Lettings business but unless anyone made a very high offer for the whole business, which he said was extremely doubtful in this market, he warned there would be no money for the creditors. Which as far as I was concerned meant me.

Checklist:

1. If you have to attend any kind of meeting like the creditors' meeting above where there is no legal reason for a solicitor to be present, don't cut corners. Pay up. The moral support is worth their fee, let alone if they happen to be called upon for some legal issue.

2. Don't be surprised if you get no worthwhile return as a result of the liquidation process. The bank *always* comes first, and usually there will be several, or dozens of people before you in the queue, if indeed there's anything in the pot to begin with.

TWENTY-FOUR

Buying back the business

If one more person says to me, 'Well, you must have only paid peanuts for it', I shall scream. Richard and I paid a lot of money to buy back the business, but at least we had the furniture, computers and other equipment, a ton of stationery (they obviously loved ordering stuff and five years on we still haven't used up all the envelopes), and the logo.

But what a hateful experience, dealing with the liquidators.

We were advised to go to the bank they used, which coincidentally was the same as mine. I thought that would be an advantage as I was such a long-standing customer. Wrong.

Three men, two of them very young, sat around a table opposite Richard and me. They gave us their business cards and I noticed one was a liquidator who would be liaising with Andrew Gastone. One of the young ones – I forget what his title was, but something along the lines of Business Co-ordinator – took out his mobile phone and laid it on the table, its lights gleaming.

'I'm sorry to have to leave my mobile on,' he apologised, 'but my wife is about to give birth at any moment.'

Great. He'll really be concentrating on the matter in hand.

I waited for one of them to say something. No one spoke, not even to state the reason we were all there.

'So shall we kick off the meeting,' I said, 'by asking what sort of figure you're looking for?'

The three men glanced at one another as though surprised I should be so blunt. Then the senior man said, 'We suggest somewhere in the region of £300,000.'

Richard and I shot a look at one another, our mouths open in disbelief.

'That's for the whole chain, of course,' the senior man added.

'Oh, of course,' I said, not hiding my sarcasm. 'How did you work out that valuation?' I was genuinely curious.

'Well, there's still a pipeline of actual exchanges,' he answered, 'and also a substantial amount of sales agreed.'

'Any of which could collapse at a moment's notice,' I said, 'especially when there's been no one to nurse them through. That's the trickiest part of the transaction, which no one ever realises. So what else?'

'There's the goodwill,' the second young man said. I looked at him. No, he wasn't being ironical.

'Do you not understand what's happened?' I asked, already getting agitated. 'Your two *customers*, who the bank thought so much of, even though I warned Mr Chakrajevan on two occasions what cheats they were, have destroyed what you know by your records was a thriving and successful business when it was managed by me. There is *no* goodwill left.'

'I was working in the company until it went bust,' Richard interjected. 'It was only the staff who kept it going. The management was worse than useless. Our reputation was going downhill by the week.'

The meeting ran on a bit longer and Richard and I said we'd come back to them with an offer more appropriate to a business that had been ruined. They told us to get in touch with Andrew Gastone direct.

We made him an offer. He refused. We offered more. He refused again. We doubled it on a third and final time. We were kept waiting for a month for his response. I wondered if he was dragging it out on purpose, forcing us to up our offer, but we couldn't go any higher. It was incredibly frustrating because we wanted to get the new business up and running as seamlessly as possible while our old sellers were still current, as we were hoping to regain their instructions.

After a few more weeks Andrew Gastone accepted our offer but would not include Residential Lettings. He said he was going to sell it separately and that someone had already made an offer of £40,000 for it without even seeing the books. More fool them.

We could ill afford our offer which Andrew Gastone had finally agreed to, but just hoped the properties which were ready to exchange would actually do so. At least they would then offset some of the purchase price of the business.

Richard and I were in the graphic artist's office one morning looking at logos and colours for the new company, rather on edge, knowing contracts were going to exchange at any moment. Mind you, we were supposed to have exchanged the day before. But at the last minute we found they hadn't included one of the villages. Even though Colin had closed it, it was still part of the chain. Richard and I only intended to open the two branches but we needed to buy all the elements of the original business so we were in full control. Mark had now managed to sort this out.

My mobile rang. It was Andrew. Thank goodness. I felt a little rise of excitement pulse through me that we were going to exchange contracts. Finally, after all this time, we'd be able to get started – pick up the pieces. Richard looked across at me with raised eyebrows. I mouthed Andrew's name.

'We're just about ready to exchange contracts,' Andrew said.

'Good.' I smiled into the phone.

'But before we do, I'm putting your deposit on hold.'

My heart somersaulted. I had a horrible feeling something wasn't right. 'Why?' I tried to keep the panic from my voice.

'I've heard from our solicitors. They asked me whether I realised there were several substantial exchanges that are due next week.'

'There are always exchanges due no matter what date,' I said. But I knew what was coming.

'We will have to slightly renegotiate.'

'What sort of slight renegotiation?' Out of the corner of my eye I saw Richard's optimistic expression change to concern.

'We'll share the exchanges 50/50 for the first four weeks, then 75 per cent to you and 25 per cent to us after a month. This is provided you do the work to see them through,' he said smoothly, as though it was a perfectly reasonable offer.

I was totally unprepared for such a change at this last minute. Andrew Gastone knew what misery I'd been through with people not keeping their word.

'This is completely different from our verbal agreement,' I argued. 'The exchanges were part of our calculations when we upped our offer.'

'Take it or leave it,' was the curt reply. 'It's that, or we don't proceed.'

'We voted for you to take over this case because of your national reputation,' I said, my voice cool, 'and you're now acting totally unprofessionally. The contract actually says the exchanges will all be ours.'

'There's too much money involved. And your offer was very low.'

'Then you shouldn't have accepted it.'

Furious, I tried to meet halfway but he wouldn't budge.

'I need to speak to Richard and our solicitor,' I said. 'I'll come back to you.'

I was beginning to feel that no one could be trusted. Professionals reneged on deals and changed the agreed terms at the last minute, even when hands were shaken.

When would I ever learn?

If we wanted to proceed we had to accept the new conditions but it meant that we'd offered far too much for the business when we'd relied on the property exchanges coming through.

I rang Mark. He was disgusted.

'They're holding a gun to your head,' he said. 'You've just got to decide whether it's worth it to you.'

After some discussion Richard and I decided to carry on. I rang Andrew back.

'We're not happy, but we'll go ahead.'

'Excellent,' he said, in a tone that told me it was nothing less than he'd expected. 'By the way, the cheques for the whole percentage of commission will be made out to us and we'll forward on your share after it clears with the bank.'

In other words the liquidators were taking charge even though we'd be doing all the work.

Just as we predicted we ended up spending a huge amount of time on those vendors' files. We rang each vendor trying to persuade them they must, by law, honour their original contract to DB Estates to sell their property. DB Estates had produced their buyer who had gone through to completion of the purchase. We explained we were the new company who had bought DB Estates, and even though the name had changed we were entitled to the commission. As you can imagine, people were reluctant to pay up. They argued that as DB Estates had folded they didn't have any obligation towards it.

In a way you couldn't blame them. Two or three threatened they would get their solicitor on to us and report us to the National Association of Estate Agents. The liquidators had to get their own solicitors on to the remaining few stubborn cases and many months went by before they all paid up.

The liquidators dribbled through the cheques representing commissions due to us, usually taking weeks after they'd received theirs. We were constantly chasing them, which didn't bode well for the best relationship. It was such a relief when they paid us the last cheque and we could carry on the business without having to deal with that company again.

It's difficult to describe my feelings at the time. Loving a challenge, I often found myself really enthusiastic and excited at starting another venture. The world of business always fascinates me, and having learned everything I knew by my own mistakes and experience it was fun having a fresh start and sharing it this time with a business partner. But the other part of me felt nervous and sick with worry that I was doing the wrong thing at the wrong time of my life in certainly what was to prove the worst market I've ever worked in. At the best of times you need real drive and energy to start up a company and I wasn't sure I could dredge it up again. But I was in it now, for good or bad, and there was another person relying on me to contribute both financially and physically to make sure it was a success. I couldn't let Richard down.

Anthony Bradshaw was back on the scene again. Remember him? The one who gave me the first offer of a million, and then made some rather onerous terms. We'd kept in touch periodically, as he was disappointed I'd sold to two incompetents, as he called them. He always said he didn't see it working and that if there was any sign they were going downhill, to let him know – he would still be most interested.

'One of my former managers and I have bought the business back,' I told him in our latest phone conversation, and explained we were only going to open up two offices, as not only was money a consideration, but we didn't want to spread ourselves too thinly.

'Why don't you come down to the coast and see me,' he suggested. 'I've bought an estate agency in which I'm actually hands-on ... with a partner. Maybe we can pool our resources.'

'You don't have any experience of estate agency,' I said.

'I'm picking it up fast,' he answered.

Amazing how everyone thinks they can be an estate agent with no training. I just wish would-be estate agents had to study and go through formal exams, then get a licence as you have to in the US. It takes two years in some states, whereas homeowners in the UK happily trust someone to value their house, not knowing if they were an egg salesman the week before (I actually knew of such a person) and the following week announce to the world they are a senior negotiator. And all at the unsuspecting public's expense. No wonder estate agents are given such bad press.

Neither Richard nor I were interested in having a third party join us but we were curious as to what he'd bought and how it was presented. Maybe we could pick up a few tips. After a pleasant drive to the coast we found his office – well, it found us. It was painted a 'hit-you-between-the-eyes' scarlet, and the interior was just as red and glaring.

Anthony and his partner showed us around. It was all very high tech. The core of the business was downstairs in the cellar, which had been made into a marvellous work station for about ten negotiators. They were so focused on their phone calls

and computers they hardly glanced up, but when we spoke
to a couple of them it was apparent how much they enjoyed
their work.

Back upstairs it was all reception bar, sofas, tables and chairs,
and huge screens which the would-be buyers could log into and
find their dream home. A mineral-water machine leaned against
one wall, and two girls with big hair and serious make-up kept
a sharp eye on any punter walking through the door. They
would immediately acknowledge the person with a smile and
a cheery greeting and offer a cup of coffee. Impressive.

We were suitably dazzled by it all, but when driving back and
discussing their venture we unanimously agreed it was not the
sort of agency we would want to set up. It was probably fine for
their area – they did appear extremely successful – but we didn't
think our town was ready for anything quite that extreme.

We decided to use our surnames for the new company. People
knew us in the estate agency world so it made sense to trade
on our own names. The next step was to contact several of my
ex-employees we thought would be interested. Unsurprisingly,
they were thrilled to hear our news. After some rapid interviews we hired all of them. We wished we could have taken
on all the original staff, but opening only two offices greatly
restricted us.

We opened on 4 July, Independence Day, complete with the
independent black cat logo which we thought very appropriate.

At first there was a huge amount of work to do, as there
always is with a new business, but in the meantime the housing
market began to crumble around us. We would sit for hours
with no phone calls. I was forever picking up the receiver,
checking that the lines hadn't been cut, but there was usually
the purr of the dialling tone.

I say 'usually' because we were actually cut off by the phone company at least half a dozen times between the two offices in the first year. Each time we worried ourselves sick that the public would think we must not have paid our bills and be reluctant to instruct us on their property in case we were about to go down the chute for the second time. In fact we did have several complaints from the public who were trying to get through and received a voice message saying the line was no longer in use.

The phone company was in a complete muddle, getting us confused with DB Estates who were, surprise surprise, behind with their payments. Richard and I went nearly crazy each time it happened. It took a month before they believed us, that we were no longer DB Estates, and any outstanding bills were not ours. Reluctantly they would send someone out to reconnect us.

The trouble is that when you ring these phone companies you speak to a different person each time, and although they are polite and even sympathetic, they have little clout to do anything. The ombudsmen for such companies were a joke. It seemed they could do nothing and didn't want to bother themselves anyway. We ended up claiming £19,000 for estimated loss of business and reputation. After several months we were offered £500 and barely a hint of apology, even though on two or three points they actually admitted they were at fault or there'd been an oversight. It was an insult, and we turned it down, still hoping we could get compensation more in proportion to our losses. We never did. And we never got the £500 either.

We spent the days contacting all our old clients and felt ourselves very busy, but at the end of the first six months we realised we'd brought in practically nothing except an occasional split fee with the liquidators on what should have been the outstanding exchanges we thought we'd bought in the first place.

In the meantime Mark resumed proceedings as Nigel and Colin were personal guarantors. In other words, even though they had been a limited company, the contract stated that if they went into administration or liquidation or bankruptcy, they had personally guaranteed to fulfil their financial obligations to me.

Mark did his best to wheedle out some more money from them but to no avail. We were nearing a date to go to court but he hoped for my sake we could once and for all settle out of court.

He decided to call a telephone meeting, solicitor to solicitor, together with the judge who would be presiding that day. Mark said I could be in the room and the loudspeaker would be on so I could hear the replies of Colin and Nigel's solicitor.

The phone meeting lasted about half an hour. As usual it would have been fascinating if I hadn't been the prosecutor. Mark and the judge got along very well, and even Colin's new solicitor (Mr Fritch had refused to continue to act for him on the grounds that he hadn't been paid) sounded reasonable, but after the meeting Mark had a serious word with me.

'You know I would love to take this case to its very furthest, don't you?' His blue eyes were bright. 'We've discussed it before and I know you're keen to go ahead. But I have to warn you again of the consequences. You'll certainly win the case. It's down in black and white on your contract, and there's no argument, but they will say they have no money—'

'But we know they have – that it's most likely off-shore,' I argued.

'We don't *know* that,' he said. 'We only suspect, which is not the same. What I'm telling you is that they'll say they have no money to pay you and you'll end up with yet another large bill as we'll most certainly have to employ a barrister. Also, it's a nerve-wracking business going in the witness box—'

'I've done it several times before,' I interrupted, 'and won every time.'

'Were the cases in connection with your business?'

'Yes,' I said. 'Two of them were developers, another two were sellers—'

'Probably clear-cut cases lasting no more than an hour, with contracts to prove it,' Mark said. 'I think you'd find this very different. It will be a High Court case which could last up to a fortnight. And take up to a year to get a date.'

How could my little business be worth using up a fortnight of a judge's and barrister's time in a High Court?

'I want you to think about it very carefully over the weekend,' he said, 'and let me know how you want to proceed. But my advice is, unless you have a spare £50,000 or so knocking about, don't do it.'

I thought about it all weekend, and changed my mind a dozen times. In the end, I decided there was no point in spending another load of money I could ill afford when I still had the leases to worry about, and a new business to concentrate on in a crummy market. I rang and told him.

'I'll have one last go with them,' he said, and rang off.

He emailed me that he'd asked for an out-of-court payment of £50,000, which was a tiny fraction of what they owed me. They refused. But to my surprise they came back again. Mark rang me when I was in my favourite department store trying on clothes.

'Are you sitting down?' he asked.

There was a chair in the fitting room so I made use of it.

'They've offered £20,000 in six payments.'

'I wouldn't dream of going along with another of their payment schedules,' I told him. 'Don't they think I've learned my lesson by now?'

I didn't believe I'd get any more money but I thought I might as well humour Mark.

'Tell them I'll have two equal payments over three months,' I said, 'or I'll continue with the plan to take them to court. I shan't, but they don't know that.'

Incredibly they kept to this last agreement. Never mind that the first payment had a big chunk taken out of it by Mark's firm, the second one was intact, and I regarded it as bunce. I was still hundreds of thousands of pounds out of pocket but was nevertheless amazed at the last two cheques.

But don't you think it astonishing that Colin and Nigel could suddenly come up with what most people would regard as a substantial sum when they were supposed to be broke?

Checklist:

1. Always, *always* get a verbal agreement confirmed in writing, even when you are dealing with the professionals. Or *especially* when you are.

2. If you start up another business be very cautious about joining forces with a similar company, especially if they are new and the owner(s) has set views which don't coincide with your own. It will complicate and compromise your business and could send a mixed message to the public. Remember the golden rule: KISS (Keep it simple, stupid).

3. Court cases are stressful and extremely costly. Avoid them if you possibly can. Always try to settle out of court.

4. Some business owners have made successful claims against phone companies for cutting them off with no reason, but be aware you could spend hours and days, even weeks, trying to get the problem sorted, let alone getting any compensation.

TWENTY-FIVE

The housing market plummets

It took a while for it to sink in that I may have made a mistake by opening up again in the same village where I lived, especially as I was using my surname along with the surname of my business partner. Rumours were flying and it eventually got back to my ears that many of the villagers thought *I* had gone bankrupt. But I wasn't aware of this when we first opened the doors. People who knew me well had sent flowers and cards, and others came in to welcome me back.

'You are brave,' several of them said.

I wasn't quite sure what they meant. Yes, the market was dire but they knew I was the kind of person who was always up for a challenge. But then two or three would add a comment along the lines of, 'After all you've been through and made bankrupt, fancy even *thinking* about starting up again.' So once more I'd have to patiently explain that it wasn't *me* who'd gone into liquidation but my buyers, and that was through total incompetency and indifference to the nature of the business they'd bought. I reminded these disbelievers that I'd survived a four-year recession when I first started but didn't divulge much more than that. Gradually the villagers seemed to accept that the whole decline and fall of DB Estates had had nothing to do with me.

I did explain to a few of my old business cronies that I'd felt

forced to come back in order to pay for the leases, and then I'd
get a lot of understanding nods.

At first it was strange having to confer with someone else,
Richard, even for minor decisions, as I'd spent nearly twenty
years deciding everything on my own. I'd always relished
having complete control, not being obliged to ask anyone
else's opinion or advice, but I remembered how I'd sometimes
longed for a second opinion or someone to share the risk. Now
I had my business partner.

It was his first business so although he deferred to me quite
often in the setting up of it, he was the one who had remained
in estate agency so knew all the rules and regulations which
had come in since I'd sold three years before. I would then
defer to him. He's brilliant at keeping the books and record-
ing everything, and is the only man I've ever come across who
not only has a tidy desk but keeps his filing up to date! If I
could just read his handwriting (which beats most of his team
as well as me) I would consider us to be a perfect match. But as
you may remember, my handwriting is all over the place, so
perhaps we really *are* the perfect match.

We could tell the market was a bit shaky before Colin
and Nigel went bust, but if I'd had an inkling of how it was
hurtling towards the edge of the cliff, I would *never* have
agreed to start up again. Instructions were terribly thin on the
ground and sales almost non-existent. We just didn't have any
choice to offer anyone. And when we did manage to get a sale
going it was often stymied by the mortgage lenders simply
not lending. If it wasn't them it was the surveyors, terrified
of their own shadows and the market dropping even further.
They would value the property right down, even though they
had no evidence that their figure was fair. In the end you'd
have another frustrated seller and another upset buyer. Each

time this happened it was one more transaction which we were counting on down the drain. Almost as bad as seeing our commission fly out of the window was how upsetting it was for our morale. But we had to put an optimistic face on for the staff, and indeed anyone thinking of selling their home.

We had a strong team in both branches though I was worried about the number of staff in the town office. It seemed we had taken on far too many for a start-up in what we could already tell was going to be a challenging market.

Of course we'd calculated there'd be no money coming in for the first three months as there's a time lag for the solicitors to prepare the legal contract, and mortgage lenders to check the finances. But six months down the line we realised we were heading for financial disaster. The figures were appalling. There were no first-time buyers at all as few young people could manage the 25 per cent deposit unless their parents coughed up. This percentage was the new deposit the banks were looking for. It was a massive change from the 0 to 10 per cent of the 'old days'. Hardly anyone was moving up the ladder as people were having problems getting an increased mortgage. Lenders were mindful of so many of their clients being made redundant or the self-employed having a sharp reduction in their businesses.

We had to make an agonising decision on whether we should amalgamate the two offices, closing the one in town and working out of the village branch. The payroll was crippling us and the bank was getting twitchy. Of course, this was at the time when banks were rarely lending on new businesses (not much change there) let alone supporting them through a rocky period. And as we were not using my old bank – I was too disgusted with them – the new bank manager didn't know me in the same way.

'So what would be your advice?' Richard and I asked our bank manager after discussing the situation and putting all the possibilities in front of him.

'I think you're wise to close one of the offices,' he said. 'It's a great pity but you're not the only ones who are having to cut your losses.' He pressed his glasses back up on the bridge of his nose. 'It could be worse.' He gave a sympathetic smile.

After another couple of months of hardly any revenue I was on the verge of packing in the whole company, though I'm not sure Richard was quite at that stage. Yet I hated to think it had beaten me. There must be a way out. And of course Richard needed the business as much as I did.

We sought advice from Peter at Business Link (set up as a free advice bureau for independent entrepreneurs during Margaret Thatcher's government – unfortunately Business Link is no longer in operation). We told him the bank manager had urged us to bring the town office into the village office as at least I owned the building and we wouldn't need to pay any rent at all until we got back on our feet. Peter looked at the first-year accounts (representing nine months) and said it made sense as there was very little in the pipeline and therefore very little cash to expect. He listened to all we had to say and then took us by surprise.

'My head tells me you should amalgamate the two offices but my heart says you should soldier on for another three months, although you'll have to cut down the staff with immediate effect.'

By this time Richard and I had agreed between ourselves we would try to hang on a bit longer, so it was great that our business consultant had reached the same conclusion. It certainly inspired us not to panic into taking such a drastic step so soon.

Another month went by but it was no better.

'We can't go on throwing good money after bad,' I told Richard. 'I think we have to take the decision to close our office in town. The sooner the better.'

I hated even voicing the words. It felt so alien to my usual optimistic outlook, and I didn't relish the idea of coming away as a *real* failure this time. We really did have the present critical economy to blame, but nevertheless, it was galling to admit defeat.

'Let's wait a bit,' Richard answered unexpectedly. I'd been so sure he would agree with me. 'I think it's about to turn the corner. I've got a few sales about to go through. Let's review it in two months. Then we'll cut straight away, if necessary.'

If he still wanted to take the chance then I'd go along with him. In a funny way I really respected him for persuading me to keep going. It would have been awful to have got tied in with a weak business partner.

In the end we kept both branches but regretfully we had to lose three of our town employees. It was embarrassing for us but terrible for them as it was the second time they'd lost their jobs in less than a year. Also, of course, those in the village office were worried they might be next. But we all pulled together and worked hard in a worsening market. Everyone took a pay cut and no commission with the promise of a review in a year. They really were fantastic. No moans and groans. I think they felt grateful they still had a job and the challenge of really making it work again.

The annoying thing was that the landlord of the town office had had no inkling of the possibility of our closing it. Instead of being satisfied with good tenants in such a bad economic climate he suddenly doubled the rent. Why any landlord would do that is beyond me. Greed, I suppose.

We realised we would definitely not be able to keep that office going, but then we had our first piece of luck. My old Residential Lettings office just up the road had become a private finance company during the time of DB Estates, and the chaps who leased the premises said they only needed a presence. They asked if we would like to take over the major share of the footage and utilities and they would just keep a desk for occasional use.

We grabbed at the opportunity as it was about half what we'd been paying, therefore only a quarter of the new rent our present landlord was demanding. We gave notice to him and within a fortnight had moved back to the old Lettings office. This just happened to be my sales office back in the 1990s when Richard had left his company and come to work for me to open up the new branch. So in a way, we'd gone full circle and were back 'home'.

We rarely saw anything of the financial service chaps and not much more than a year later they assigned the whole of the lease over to us. We even have the original elderly landlords (who are lovely) from when I first opened that office fifteen years ago.

Needless to say, the landlord who'd said he was doubling our rent had a To Let sign up on his premises for a very long time.

Word seemed to have got round both in the business and private sectors that the two of us were back in our respective offices, and the company was definitely here to stay. A few more instructions started to dribble in.

We badly needed new stock. We rang all the solicitors we used to deal with and a couple of them gave us two or three welcome probates. But it wasn't enough.

'Isn't it about time you moved, Anna?' I asked my sister one day.

'Funnily enough I've been vaguely thinking about it,' she said, to my delight.

Anna loves moving. Even in such a rotten market we sold her Victorian townhouse easily. Five people were practically fighting over it and it went way over the advertised price, mainly because of her interior decorating skills. She ended up buying a 'to do up' property through our company and has since moved yet again, both buying and selling through us. To this day she takes full credit for giving our business the kick-start it needed!

Gradually we built up some sales followed by the odd day when the postman would deliver a cheque or three. Our boards began to pepper the streets, which sometimes galvanised a neighbour into deciding it was time for *them* to move. After three months we knew we'd made the right decision to keep both branches going. We'd won through. We were going to be all right. And although we lost a fair amount of money that first year and we had to throw some more in the coffers, we made a very respectable profit in year two. We were thrilled and took everyone out to dinner to celebrate.

Checklist:

1. When you start, or re-start, a new business, set it up with the absolute minimum number of staff. It's easy to add extra staff, but highly embarrassing for you and upsetting for them if you have to make them redundant because you took on too many in the first place. You just have to remind yourself that as the owner you need to work twice as hard as you would for an employer.

2. Keep an eye on the advertising. This is often your second major expense after salaries in a variety of businesses.

3. Look at any purchase you wish to make such as computer software, stationery, printing etc. Get various quotes. The business doesn't need luxuries and can be built up gradually. This is particularly important in a poor economy.

4. Take professional advice *well* before the business goes pear-shaped. Quite often another pair of eyes can see things you can't. I can't state enough what a valuable exercise this is, even though you now have to pay for it.

TWENTY-SIX

Tackling the leases

But what was the latest with Colin and Nigel?

By chance I'd been invited to a rather posh wine-tasting lunch and met up with a business acquaintance who is a multi-millionaire. We sat next to one another and he asked me why I'd gone back into business. I told him the whole sorry story and after the lunch I gave him a lift to the station. (Yes, even multi-millionaires have to cadge a lift sometimes.) He immediately got on to his mobile and spoke to a business friend who he said would help me. Apparently, the chap was a top investigator. He arranged for the two of us to meet in a few days' time at one of his restaurants.

The investigator, Robert O'Brien, was an older man who looked ready for retirement. Coincidentally, he worked for the same liquidators used to wind up DB Estates and was most interested in my account.

'Are they going to get away with it?' I asked him, pandering to his ego to take up the challenge.

'Not if I have anything to do with it,' he said, 'and seeing as how I've been assigned to the case, it's very unlikely. I've already begun the investigation.'

'That's great news,' I said. 'I'd love to work with you to make them face up to their responsibilities. They've upset so many people's lives and businesses.'

'Well, any information you get, ring me. You can be sure the bank won't let up either.' He took several gulps of coffee. 'Did you know the bank closed down their site when they tried to start up another business?'

'Only because I warned them what was going on,' I told him. 'It wouldn't have happened otherwise.'

He looked suitably impressed.

'Will the bank go after them for their money?' I asked.

'Without a doubt,' he said. 'They won't let that slip through.'

'But do you know the latest?' I said. Mr O'Brien drained his coffee and leaned forward. 'Colin has opened yet another web-based estate agency, but this time behind his old business consultant, Dave Crannerley. It's under Dave's name, or rather his son's, so the bank can't do anything about it as it's not Dave they're after. But it's dreadful that the public don't know what or who's behind the company, especially as they wrote in their blurb that estate agents haven't always had the best reputation but that this new company comprises (and I quote) *honest, open and experienced agents who would deliver the top service*.'

'I'll look into that one,' he promised, and jotted down a few notes.

'And when you think that neither of them had ever even accompanied anyone on a valuation let alone told someone what their house is worth. Or took on a property and negoti-ated a sale. You can't believe the sheer arrogance.'

Robert (he'd asked me to call him) nodded in agreement. He said he would stay in touch and gave me his card. I climbed into my Mini, not believing my luck that I'd finally latched on to someone employed as a detective who was really going to make them pay.

Mark was delighted that an investigator was on the case.

'Phone me with any news,' he said.

‡

The next time I phoned Robert I told him I knew on the best authority there was money around even though Colin and Nigel had always professed to have none. I decided not to tell him Colin had sent me those two cheques. I didn't want to put my little unexpected windfall into any kind of jeopardy.

'I'm positive they've put a lot of money off-shore,' I told him. 'There was too much money coming in that was unaccounted for, but so far as I know this has never been chased.'

'It's easier to find off-shore accounts these days,' Robert said. 'People can't get away with it like they used to in the old days. Oh, no, we'll be on to that, you can bet your life.'

My heart did a little leap. He sounded dead serious; he was really going to track them down. And he assured me they'd get their just deserts.

'They both own their properties,' I told him. 'Even though Colin lied when he warned me in the early days it was no good my looking to Nigel for any money – that Nigel didn't own his house but rented it from Colin's mother. But I've had it confirmed on Land Registry that Nigel *does* own his own home.'

'That's interesting.'

'Can they be made to sell their properties and pay back their creditors?' I asked.

'Most definitely. But don't get too excited – the bank will have first call.'

He promised to keep me posted.

However, the next time I rang to ask if there were any developments, I picked up a distinctly chilly tone to his voice. Either he resented being chased by me or he had gone off the idea of nabbing them and had a new, more exciting, case to deal with.

Worse, maybe he'd been told by the liquidators it wasn't worth investigating them after all.

Once more I felt let down. If Colin and Nigel were never pursued by the bank or the liquidator, or indeed the law, they would have got clean away with it. It was a depressing thought.

With frightening regularity demands for the rents of all the previous office premises kept coming through at the same time as Richard and I were trying to establish the new business. I was responsible for five buildings and needed to off-load them pronto.

I asked a local solicitor, Graham Brand, who specialised in commercial leases, if he could help. He looked through all the leases and contracts very carefully and said there might be a way out for some of them. He explained that the law had changed since I took over my first lease twenty years ago, and it was to the *possible* benefit of the tenant. In essence, it all depended on how eagle-eyed the solicitor on the landlord's side was. If they had their wits about them they would spot the clause on the changeover (i.e. from Colin and Nigel back to me), that *unless the landlord's solicitor served notice on the guarantor* (me) *within a certain length of time* (usually six months, but it could be shorter or longer) *to say that the guarantor had to continue liability on the lease, then it would be null and void.*

'Surely all the solicitors know about this,' I said, not very hopeful.

'Not necessarily,' Graham answered. 'It's a newish law and they might inadvertently overlook it.'

And do you know – two of them didn't spot it and let the time limit lapse. A third landlord said he was going to take back the premises for his own use (hurrah!) and a fourth changed the building into a shop[†] below and a separate flat above, thereby instantly negating the terms of the lease. (That was the most expensive lease, and the relief I felt was indescribable.) As for the fifth, well, the landlord (a very shrewd professional) must have known the terms by heart and his solicitor served notice on me. So I remain responsible for one out of the five – which is pretty good, considering.

But one of the landlords, Barry, was furious because I refused to continue paying for his empty premises. I explained that his solicitor should have served notice on me but Barry wouldn't have it. He began to phone me every few days.

'I insist that you pay me, Denise,' he would say. 'You're responsible, and you're in business again, which is not doing anything for your reputation.'

Here we go again.

I would explain yet again, but after a few more calls he began to get threatening.

'I'm afraid I will have to take you to court. Nothing personal, you understand. Simply business.'

What a relief that I shouldn't be taking it personally.

'Look, Barry,' I said, 'my solicitor tells me I don't have to pay you, and yours says I do. One of them is right and one of them is wrong. I think mine is right and I'm paying him, so I'd be pretty stupid not to take his advice.'

'Well, I have the best solicitor in the country, and he says you *do* owe it.'

'Even the best solicitor in the country can make a mistake,' I retorted. 'Sorry, Barry, but you'll have to take me to court,

---

† To my delight, this was eventually leased to Farrow & Ball. I would have been most upset if it had been taken by another estate agent. And when I look up to the first floor which was my old Country Homes department, there on the window is the white etching I'd had made of my cat logo. It always makes me smile as I walk by.

because I'm not going to pay unless my solicitor says he's made a mistake. And he's adamant that he's right and I don't owe you anything.'

Barry slammed the phone down on me.

Of course I reported all this to Graham, but he told me not to worry. The clause was clear in black and white. Meanwhile the commercial agent had found new tenants for the fifth office where I am still head lessee. Two chaps took it over who were looking to expand. I've never met them but have read about them in their brochure as they do charity work in Third World countries. They sounded so nice I took them on, and have had no problems at all. They pay the rent (under the exact terms of my lease) direct to the landlord, and I only have two more years left to go before I am totally off the hook. Lovely tenants though they are, I'll still feel happier when the time comes that I can relinquish that final responsibility.

Three months after Barry had hung up on me he strode into my office. He was a big man and quite intimidating. My heart beat hard. I just knew he was going to make a scene and was thankful we didn't have any clients listening in. I glanced round at the staff. They'd managed to suddenly become extraordinarily busy picking up phones to make what I am sure were spurious calls. Outwardly, I kept calm.

'I just wanted to say that your solicitor was right.' Barry's expression dissolved into what can only be described as sheepish.

Good God. That must have cost him something. The girls all put down their receivers at the same time, just like Nora Batty and her cronies with their cups and saucers in *Last of the Summer Wine*. My lot weren't going to miss this one.

'I had every confidence in him,' I said, trying not to sound too smug, 'but you threw me a bit when you said you had the best solicitor in the country.'

'Hmm. I understood he was. Anyway,' Barry suddenly smiled, 'there's no hard feelings between us any more, is there?'

I assured him there wasn't, indeed, that there never had been. And we shook hands.

'But I can tell you something,' he shot over his shoulder as he made to leave. 'I'm suing *my* solicitor instead!'

Checklist:

1. Be aware that just because someone has professional credentials and says they want to help does not necessarily mean they will. They may start with the best intentions but find later that fulfilling them proves to be impossible. Or they may be pumping you for information and then have no more need of you.

2. When things look financially gloomy in your business, take advice from your bank manager, your accountant and your business partner, but in the end don't make a hasty decision. Take your time, especially when it's down to whether the business keeps running or you have to fold it. If you are short of funds ask family and friends if they would contribute. If the cost is spread, they might well help with a modest cheque. The turning of the corner might just be ... well, around the corner.

3. Never be intimidated by threats from a customer, landlord, member of staff etc. If you are sure you are in the right just reiterate your position, be scrupulously polite, but do make sure you're on solid ground.

TWENTY-SEVEN

Abandoned files in moonlight flit

I decided to bring Alan Dorrinne (remember my good-looking business agent?) up to date. He sounded pleased to hear from me until I told him I wanted to see him. Then he went a bit quiet.

'Anything in particular?' he asked, sounding wary.

'I want to bring you up to date with all that's been happening this past year,' was all I said.

We arranged to meet in one of the local pubs for lunch.

Only the waiter interrupted us as I filled Alan in with the details.

'I really thought they'd make a go of it,' he said, lifting his eyes from his plate.

'Did you vet them at all?'

This was the second time I'd asked this question. The first time I never managed to get an answer.

'In what way?'

I could tell by his tone that he didn't like the question this time around either.

'Financially,' I said. 'Whether they owned their own houses; how much money they were each putting into the business – as I told you, Nigel only contributed £2,500. What their financial history was. Crucial things that would have had a bearing on whether I sold to them or not.' I hoped I didn't sound too confrontational.

'As far as the finances go, that's the job of the lenders.'

I was stunned. In all the brochures I'd read about business selling agents, vetting the proposed buyers for their financial background was one of the main features of their service. Had I really skipped over any warning in the contract that Alan's company didn't look into the financial affairs of anyone showing interest?

'I assumed that by paying your commission of 3.5 per cent you would have done that. Even we estate agents look into people's financial situation as far as we're able, and ask for proof if we're not happy – and we charge a much lower commission.'

'We don't interfere with that side,' Alan said firmly. 'It's for the bank to do.'

'OK, leaving aside their actual financial ability, or lack of,' I said, warming to my theme, 'you can't deny it was your job to find out more about them – their backgrounds, whether Nigel was really a qualified chartered surveyor, whether they owned their properties, if Colin really had a business the size of mine, as he told me he'd had, and subsequently sold. I've since found out plenty of stuff about those two. Colin never did own his own business – someone told me he worked for a second-hand car dealer. It all fits in.' I kept my voice level. Alan had the grace to look abashed.

'And the two of them never did fall out,' I continued. 'That was just a ploy to make it look authentic that Nigel was supposedly driven out of the partnership. That's why Colin agreed to Nigel only putting peanuts into the business in the first place. They both knew Nigel wouldn't be a director for long. And Colin knew I'd never sell him the business if I'd thought he was on his own. He even asked me once if I would have and I told him no, and he said he knew that's what I'd say. And not only are they still friends, they still work together.'

'How did you find that out?'

'One of the staff told me Colin used Nigel to do surveys after he was supposed to have walked out, dissolving the partnership. And they planned all along not to pay me my full money and to use the warranties as an excuse. So of course Nigel wasn't going to inspect the buildings before the exchange of contracts as he wouldn't have had any case at all.'

'Which brings me back to the fact that I don't think you made any proper checks on them.'

Alan had very little to add to that.

Then I came to the real purpose of the meeting. I'm sure he knew what was coming as he didn't appear at all surprised.

'The £42,000 I paid you was based on an estimated million.'

'Six thousand of that was VAT,' Alan interrupted.

'So you *only* got £36,000 from me for your company,' I said, 'which was the full estimated amount, but I barely got two-thirds from them. If they'd offered me that much at the beginning I would have told them to go take a jump.' Alan swallowed a mouthful of wine. 'Not much from a business that you initially valued for £1.75 million. And taking into account the huge amounts I spent trying to get what they owed me I think I'm entitled to some compensation from your company.'

'I'll see what I can do,' he said, and we finished lunch with little further conversation.

A couple of days later Alan rang.

'I've looked through the paperwork,' he said, 'and you're not entitled to any refund.'

'But the commission was on the eventual sale price which didn't materialise,' I argued.

'It's always difficult to calculate on a payment schedule.'

'You didn't point that out to me,' I said. 'It's the opposite to how estate agents invoice their clients. We get our commission based on the exact amount the house sells for, even if there was any renegotiation and the house price was reduced at the last minute. I assumed it was the same when you sold a business.'

'It's all in the contract.' His voice had lost some of its usual friendly tone.

'On the grounds of not giving me good advice or doing your job properly, don't you think I should have *some* reimbursement?' I persisted. 'Even as a goodwill gesture.'

'I wouldn't be able to do that as I don't agree you didn't get a good service.'

I was beside myself with disbelief. Was that the way he thought you should treat a client? The way to maintain your reputation? But how did I really know what reputation they had? I never spoke to anyone else who had sold their business through them. I thought of my own business. If we ever got a legitimate complaint I would always make it up to the client somehow – usually by reducing our commission, whether or not they'd asked me to. That way, we'd all end on good terms. To me, that's the right way to succeed – to admit when you're wrong. But Alan just couldn't.

'Is that all you have to say?' I asked.

'I'm sorry.'

And that was the end of the conversation.

It was months later when I thought about Alan's response coolly and calmly and realised I only had myself to blame. I hadn't read the contract thoroughly. (If you remember, I signed up with him there and then instead of taking it home and studying it properly.) It wasn't Alan's or his company's fault that I didn't take Colin and Nigel to court where there might have been a chance that I would have retrieved some of my money, so I suppose it was illogical to think he should have made some reimbursement for the shortfall.

One evening, as a director of the new business with Richard, I went along to a Chamber of Commerce meeting. Well, it would be better described as a party and it was great fun as there were lots of familiar faces. They wanted to know how the new estate agency was going, and seemed genuinely pleased we were doing well in what was still a difficult market.

One chap was there who I used to joke with when I first started my own company. I used to say he was my role model. Charles had his own chain of estate agents, set up years before me, though it was only half the size of mine. He'd sold out to his managers not long after I'd sold. Taller than many of the others, Charles caught my eye, smiled, and wended his way through the crowds to talk to me.

'I was sorry you let your business go to that pair,' he said, after kissing my cheek. 'They wanted to buy *my* company but I didn't trust them as far as I could throw them.'

He was the very person Colin and Nigel had told me about during our first meetings. I thought it might be a good opportunity to mention it.

'Yes, they told me they'd made you an offer,' I said.

'It was a stupid offer and I didn't accept it.'

'That's not quite their story.' By now, I'd really got his attention.

'Oh?'

'They said you accepted it, but just as it was about to exchange you suddenly upped the price and they had to walk away. They seemed very peeved about it and said you were unethical and unprofessional.'

Charles threw back his head and roared.

'They're a couple of chancers,' he said. 'I could tell they didn't have any money to back them by their continuous bragging. I looked into them. (More than Alan Dorrinne had done, I thought.) A load of hot air – both of them.'

'I wish I'd known.'

He looked down at me. 'I wanted to tell you … warn you … when I found out who you were selling to, but it was too late … you'd already completed on the deal. I just hoped they'd honour it.'

'They wouldn't know the meaning of the word.'

'So what happened, exactly?'

'We're supposed to be making small talk,' I laughed, looking round at the various groups of Chamber members all chatting happily away, 'but I'll give you a flavour.' And I proceeded to tell him some of the horrors.

'It's unbelievable. You know what – you should write a book.'

I smiled. 'Funny you should say that.'

He winked. 'I shall be *most* interested.'

'What I *should* have done was called *you*,' I told him. 'I nearly did; then I thought … well, you know agents … all in competition with one another. And I didn't want you to think I couldn't handle the sale of my own company.'

'I wouldn't have thought anything of the kind,' he said. 'It's a tricky thing, selling a business. Especially when you've never done it before. But you probably wouldn't have taken any notice of me anyway.'

'Maybe not. I was absolutely desperate to sell, and that's not a good place to start.'

'Well, it's all life's experiences,' he said sympathetically. 'And you've got a good business going now with Richard.'

I agreed, and on that happier note I circulated around the room.

‡

Liz told us an amusing story not long after she began working for Richard and me. She was in town driving her 4x4, which pretty much overpowers most vehicles by its sheer bulk, and happened to glance in the mirror to see what was behind her as she pulled up at the traffic lights.

And there in the mirror, two cars behind in another lane, was a beautiful silver Porsche. She looked idly to see who the driver was. You've got it: Colin. He was desperately trying to weave in and out of the traffic to change lanes but no one would let him in. Liz said there was no way she was going to. He tried so hard to zoom in front but in the end he gave up and she saw him throw both his arms up in the air in frustration. She couldn't help grinning as she put her foot down and roared away.

But a Porsche? True to form he was once again 'the big I am' behind that wheel. Was the silver dream his? Or was it rented? Or borrowed? Or…? I'll never know. But he obviously isn't short of a bob or two whichever way you look at it.

When Richard and I had first taken back the business we had to clear all the offices. It was difficult to open the shop door of my old head office with the mountain of post jammed on the other side, but eventually we pushed our way in.

'The place looks as if it's been vandalised.' Richard stooped to pick up the pile of envelopes and leaflets which appeared to be mainly junk.

I looked round what was once a beautiful office – different

from all the other agents on the high street. On the wall opposite the door as you came in used to be the stunning mural I'd
had specially painted. It was a *trompe l'oeil* of a French chateau
in the country with a black cat strolling down the lane. People
never stopped complimenting us. But as soon as Colin and
Nigel had taken command, and ignoring the protests of the
girls who worked there, they slapped a couple of coats of
magnolia over the top.

Now, in its place were bare walls with pictures torn off the
hooks. Desks and chairs had been overturned, filing cabinets were
flung open, and waste-paper baskets had spilled their contents on
the floor to join a couple of stained coffee mugs and someone's
umbrella. Telephones had been pulled out of their sockets and
none of the computers were in sight. The office smelt musty. I
shivered, imagining all the malfeasance the staff had suffered in
that room which had once had such a happy atmosphere.

We did what we could to bundle the stuff together for recy-
cling and put the furniture straight.

'Let's find out what they've done upstairs,' Richard said.

'They seem to have left in an awful hurry,' I remarked when
we reached the second floor where the boardroom was, and
my old office adjacent. Files were scattered all over the place,
papers were strewn, more chairs turned over and desk drawers
were hanging from broken hinges. The expensive and expan-
sive coffee machine, more suited to a corporate organisation,
had been left unwashed, as though Colin and Dave had only
just left the scene, their used paper cups thrown everywhere
except in the waste-paper basket.

'We must go through everything carefully,' I told Richard
when we were trying to wade through the debris. 'We might
pick up some interesting information.'

'Here's a couple of files then that you might like to look at.'
He handed me two box files, both marked DB SALE.

It was a gift.

'Oh, fantastic,' I said. 'They're bound to make fascinating
reading. And brilliant for my records.' I put them to one side,
planning to take them home to read later, though I could barely
stop myself from ripping them open straight away.

Later became a year. It took that long for me to feel in the
right frame of mind, but one day I sat down with a pot of
coffee, lifted out the two files, and went through the lot. One
thing made me smile. I had left them dozens of boxes of pink
Post-it notes which I used to give away to clients and use in
the office. My name was printed on the bottom, and every
time Colin and Nigel marked various pages in the files with
a note they used them. Fair enough. But every single one was
purposely folded and tucked underneath so my name wasn't
visible. Remember, this was just their personal files they were
keeping. Not even a member of staff would have seen them.

It was quite a novelty seeing the transaction from their
twisted viewpoints. I got towards the end, just a few weeks
before the company folded, and was turning the various letters
over when I read this email Colin had sent to his solicitor:

*Denise has popped up again. I really thought we had got rid of her.
What do we have to do now?*

It sort of reads like an Agatha Christie, doesn't it?

Checklist:

1. It's time to say again: READ THE SMALL PRINT BEFORE
   YOU SIGN ANYTHING. The smaller the print the more
   notice you should take. Always take your time to read any
   contract or legal commitment. It will be too late if you query
   the contract or other document *after* you've signed.

2. Never be too proud to ask advice of someone in the same, or
   similar, business as yourself. Most people will be flattered to
   be asked.

TWENTY-EIGHT

Smash hit!

Liz had spotted a competition, run by our local paper, *The Courier*, looking for the best estate agent in the county. She decided to put our name forward. I thought it was a great idea. When I had the original agency I went in for several competitions over the years, becoming the runner-up to the regional Businesswoman of the Year, and was twice short-listed nationally for the Best Estate Agent award. It proved a great way to advertise what outstanding agents we were.

The competition Liz had entered us in was very streamlined, running over a series of categories: the Best Independent Estate Agent, the Best Corporate, the Best Residential Lettings Agency, the Best Agent chosen by the Public, the Best Team and the Best Overall Estate Agency.

Liz spent hours of work time, home time and any other time putting the competition entry together. She decided we were eligible for four of the categories. Finally, when she'd drafted all the answers and reasons why we should win the competition, she asked me to look over it. I was amazed. It was enthusiastic, professional and clear that she and the rest of the team thought the company was the 'tops'. She had even written a very amusing poem which she also wanted to submit.

Off went the report, together with examples of our house

details, brochures and marketing material, to the newspaper. Liz also sent emails to past clients asking if they would contact the newspaper if they had been satisfied with our service.

In the meantime Richard and I carried on with the business, more or less forgetting about the competition. He was pleased Liz had entered us, but was rushed off his feet as he was doing the job of two negotiators besides being a director of a business. He badly needed a holiday – he hadn't been away at all for the last year and was working a six-day week.

Unfortunately his holiday clashed with an Arvon writing course I'd booked. We decided we had two good teams and they could manage for just a week. Until we realised the gala evening for the entrants of the competition was being held smack bang in the middle.

I was in a quandary as I thought we might have a chance of winning one of the categories. I wondered if I should cancel my course. It would be a shame if neither director was there and we won something. In the end we decided to let four of the staff, two from each office, have a table. Richard and I went on our separate holidays.

'Let me know how it all goes,' was my parting shot to Liz.

My course was great. Each evening our small group got together with wine and chatted with our tutors. On this particular evening I remembered it was the gala night for the competition so I thought I'd better check my mobile to see whether there was any news. One voice message. Liz. She sounded a little intoxicated.

'We've *won*!' her voice screamed in my ear. 'Not one, not two, but THREE prizes. Call me back, whatever time it is.'

I called her back.

'We've *won*!' she shouted again. 'Best team, best vote from the public, which is wonderful, but the most fantastic one – Best Overall Estate Agent in the county. We've beaten them all – corporates, independents, lettings … the lot!'

I couldn't believe it. Nor could I believe that neither Richard nor I had been there to enjoy the kudos of being winners for three different categories when only four of them pertained to our company anyway. And that we'd won the most important one of all. Liz said the atmosphere had been terrific. She'd given two speeches, and Monica the Lettings Manager had given one; they'd all drunk too much champagne, the applause had been deafening, and why, oh why, hadn't I been there? I was cross with myself for not thinking ahead and cancelling my course, and thrilled at the same time. Most of all I was very proud of Liz for entering us in the first place, not to mention both teams who had worked so hard in order to achieve such an accolade.

The girls were presented with three beautiful crystals with our company name etched on each and the category in which we had won. *The Courier* also gave us £5,000 worth of advertising, which was handy.

Three days later, thankfully when Richard and I were back, the newspaper wanted to write an article about the winners and take photographs. We all stood outside the village office where I'd started up all those years ago. Three of us each held up a crystal for the photo shoot. Each crystal rested in a beautiful presentation box. I tipped my box up a little further so the readers of the paper would get the full benefit.

The crystal promptly fell out of its case. It smashed to the ground. The photographer leapt back. The girls screamed in anguish. I screamed with laughter.

'If one of you had done this it would have been instant dismissal,' I said, pretending to look stern as they helped me gather up the pieces. They knew this was one of my favourite expressions that meant absolutely nothing, so of course took no notice.

In the end I managed to disguise my broken crystal by showing more of the presentation box than the content, and the photos were duly taken amid much amusement from the passers-by who were told the story. And in the newspaper photograph, snug in their satin lining, they looked like perfect triplets.

As you have to with a new business, I'd put in a lot of effort talking to as many of the villagers as I could, renewing membership of local business forums, breakfast networking; all the time spreading the word that I was back. I had to put my writing on the back burner to give this new company and my business partner the best chance. Full-time work came as a massive shock after three years of not having to turn up at the office at eight o'clock every morning. However, I got back into the routine and although it took several weeks to really settle in, it soon felt as though I'd never left.

In the second year I dropped to a four-day week, and the last few months became three. My migraines trailed off in direct proportion to my working days. I made the most of that time by writing, catching up with family and friends and dashing off to far-flung places.

My feelings were ambivalent. On the one hand I was proud to have started another business with my business partner which was already a great success, and I enjoyed the attention from the media and other business people. Winning the award of Best Estate Agent was a tremendously exciting recognition, which somehow assuaged the shame, anger and bitterness I'd felt when, having always considered myself an astute businesswoman, I'd been well and truly hoodwinked. But though it was a relief to share the stress and decisions with such a trusted and experienced estate agent as Richard, I longed for my freedom again.

It was time to break the news to Richard that the two years were up and I wanted to be gradually phased out. He tried to persuade me to carry on a further year, which was incredibly flattering, but I wanted to devote my time to writing. As I write this I am being bought out for the second time. It's as different as one end of the scale to the other: this time I have a trustworthy buyer – my business partner – who is all I could wish for. I will remain one of the two directors for a while longer, and as Richard intends to keep the name I'll always take a great interest in the company. But for now, I go to staff meetings, see old clients, value some of the more substantial properties; in other words, I keep in touch on a regular basis, but I don't have to take part in the day-to-day running of the company.

Unbelievably, we're five years down the road and it's been another profitable one considering there's such a volatile market. I was delighted to see this result was partly due to a growing number of larger houses and am hoping it won't be long before we open a special department for those top-end properties.

The sour taste has gone and it seems a long time ago that I sold out to that pair. Sometimes, as I was typing this account, my hackles would rise and my fingers would fly over the keys, recalling all their promises, and how often I fell for them. I'd be swearing under my breath as I bashed out the words. But the sickening anger and black cloud that often threatened to subsume me during my three-year 'retirement' has disappeared, just as surely as Colin and Nigel have.

‡

If you refer (constantly) to my story while in the process of
selling your business, and it stops you making any of the stupid
mistakes I made, then I will be perfectly rewarded. But if you
picked up this book out of curiosity to find out what happened
to one woman on her road to ruin – and eventual recovery –
then I hope it has entertained and inspired you.

‡

*If this book has helped you in any way, I'd love to hear from you.
Likewise, if you, by awful chance, have had a bad experience in selling
your business, I'd be very interested to know what you went through
and how you recovered. You can email me at denisebarnesuk@gmail.com
or follow me on Twitter @denisebarnesuk, and my blog is at http://
denisebarneswriter.wordpress.com.*

About the author

Denise Barnes has travelled the world, unpacking her suitcase in a score of countries and working at more jobs than she cares to remember. Mentionable ones include selling lipstick in a Denver department store, catwalk modelling in Atlanta, assistant to the UN Narcotics Director in Geneva, chauffeuring a Swiss Gnome in Zurich, assistant to an internationally famous film producer based in London, and cooking in a sanatorium in Germany, which gave rise to her first book: *From Bad to Wurst: Bavarian adventures of a veggie cook*.

Back home in England, Denise took up Britain's third most reviled profession – as an estate agent! Juggling the running of her chain of eight offices in the south-east with taking an Honours Degree with the Open University, Denise managed to pursue her lifelong passion for writing.

She sold her business in 2005 to the wrong buyers and *Seller Beware* is the result. She now has time to resume her love of fiction writing and is drafting book three of a trilogy called *The Voyagers*.

Acknowledgements

It was my sister, Carole, who worked in the company for seven years, who gave me the idea to write this book. But she had to nag, then practically bully me to finish it. The trouble was, to write it was to re-live it. But she said it was my duty to warn others about what could happen when they came to sell their business.

So I have her to thank. (Besides, she came up with the title.)

Thanks also to Edward Stanton, my husband, who set up a print room below the 'posh' office, and produced stunning house details, year on year, for the company, and when I sold was, of course, on the receiving end of my moods and misery.

To the handful of close friends and family who gave me all the love and advice (and wine!) I craved throughout the horrible three-year ordeal. Honestly, you all helped to stop me from tipping over the edge.

My heartfelt thanks go to the original women, Jean Mercer, June Pakenham and Valerie Avon, who were brave enough to leave their secure jobs and step with me into the unknown when I first started up my estate agency in June 1988. It was due to you and your sheer determination to make it work that I was able to expand to the awesome team of fifty by the time I came to sell. I wish I could have taken all fifty of you in the new business, but I'm grateful to have retained some of you. You're doing a grand job.

I must mention Howard Kingsnorth. He's made it enjoyable to be back in the world of estate agency again.

I feel lucky to have Alison Morton, alternate history thriller writer, as my eagle-eyed critique writing partner. Thank you, Alison, for your constant advice and encouragement.

And last, but definitely not least, is my Polish decorator, Kris! In a completely bizarre way he led me to my smashing publisher, Iain Dale, and editor extraordinaire, Sam Carter, and, of course, the rest of the lovely team at Biteback Publishing, a company with which I feel proud to be associated.